EMBRACING THE CALL OF God

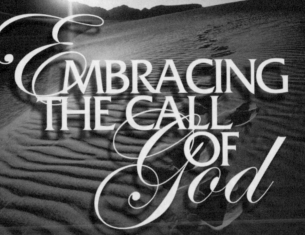

EMBRACING THE CALL OF God

FINDING OURSELVES IN GENESIS

Rick R. Marrs

COVENANT
PUBLISHING

www.covenantpublishing.com

COVENANT
P U B L I S H I N G

P.O. Box 390 Webb City, Missouri 64870
Call toll free at 877.673.1015

Library of Congress Cataloging-in-Publication Data

Marrs, Rick R.
  Embracing the call of God : finding ourselves in Genesis / Rick R. Marrs.
    p. cm.
Includes bibliographical references.
  ISBN 1-892435-25-X (pbk.)
  1. Bible. O.T. Genesis—Commentaries. I. Title.
  BS1235.53.M27 2003
  222′.1107—dc21
                        2003002391

Dedication

For Paula, Staci, and Jeremy
Through whom I daily experience God's marvelous blessings

Table of Contents

CHAPTER 1
Genesis—An Overview 11

CHAPTER 2
In the Beginning—God (Genesis 1) 25

CHAPTER 3
In the Beginning—Male and Female (Genesis 2–3) 43

CHAPTER 4
Life outside the Garden (Genesis 4–11) 61

CHAPTER 5
Embracing the Call—the Promise of Land (Genesis 12–15) 79

CHAPTER 6
Embracing the Call—the Promise of Descendants (Genesis 16–23) 97

CHAPTER 7
Will the Older Serve the Younger? (Genesis 24–28) 115

CHAPTER 8
Living a Life of Conflict (Genesis 29–36) 133

CHAPTER 9
Life In and Out of the Pit (Genesis 37–41) 153

CHAPTER 10
"You Meant to Do Me Evil; God Meant to Do Me Good"
(Genesis 42–50) 171

SUGGESTED BOOK LIST 189

ABOUT THE AUTHOR 191

Foreword

It is perhaps most fitting to begin with a short note explaining the genesis of this book on Genesis. For several years I have taken entering freshman through these marvelous materials in the Old Testament. Whether reading Genesis for the first time or the thirtieth time, the reaction is the same—students are fascinated not only by the *content* of the narratives, but also by the *manner* in which that content is communicated. However, one move regularly recurs. Students repeatedly bring their modern worldview, values, and assumptions to this ancient text. They attempt to "modernize" the ancient text, and in the process find several of the narratives difficult to maneuver. In those moments, we talk of the importance of first entering the ancient world and attempting to hear the texts of Scripture as the original audiences might have heard them. We talk of the worldview and values of the ancient Near East, and how some awareness of the ancient world often elucidates seemingly obscure passages.

This popular work results from that repeated experience. Those conversant with the scholarly discussion on Genesis will recognize my considerable indebtedness to the scholarly resources available on Genesis. However, since this is written for a popular audience, I have chosen not to provide documentation of my indebtedness to that larger scholarly discussion. For readers interested in further study, ample secondary resources are available. My hope and prayer is that readers of this work will once again return to the book of Genesis and *re*discover the wonderful theological and spiritual treasures there. As I repeatedly attempt to demonstrate, this ancient treasure is not merely ancient history; it is ultimately God's word to us—if read correctly, in these ancient narratives we see *our* story encapsulated in the message of Genesis. May God bless you in the reading and study of His Word.

Genesis provides us a theological treasure trove; it calls us to engage the most basic questions of our lives as children of God. . . . If we truly hear the message of Genesis, we soon realize that in this ancient story we hear our story; the narrative of Genesis, though far removed culturally, addresses the deepest issues of our lives.

CHAPTER 1

Genesis—
An Overview

The book of Genesis has been the subject of countless books, monographs, articles, and essays. A critic could rightly argue that sufficient ink has been spilled over Genesis; the literature is sufficient to last a lifetime. In conservative Christian circles, the relation of this ancient book to our modern world has received significant and substantial attention. Bookshelves are lined with books bringing Genesis into dialogue with such diverse topics as geology, paleontology, archaeology, biology, and history. Although these discussions are important, they are not the focus of this book. My focus is directed elsewhere; my thesis is simple. Genesis can be read profitably against a number of backdrops. The backdrop I have chosen is the ancient world; the focus I have chosen is theological. Simply put, Genesis provides us a theological treasure trove; it calls us to engage the most basic questions of our lives as children of God. It is to these questions I wish to attend.

The book of Genesis is both a theological and literary masterpiece. It is written in such a way that as believers we cannot simply read it and dismiss it as an antiquarian record of people who lived in times and places far removed from us and from the relevance of our world. If we truly hear the message of Genesis, we soon realize that in this ancient story we hear *our* story; the narrative of Genesis, though far removed culturally, addresses the deepest issues of our lives.

As students of the Word of God, we have two options before us when reading Scripture. One approach, popular and time-honored, begins by taking an ancient text of Scripture and dragging it forward into the modern world. The selected text is then read against the backdrop of 21st-century values and assumptions. Another approach, the one I have chosen for this study, involves leaving our modern world and entering the ancient world of the Bible. Although intimidating, we humbly acknowledge that the ancient texts of Scripture were not first and foremost addressed to us. They were addressed to God's ancient people; we are simply allowed to "overhear" God's word to those people. As we enter that ancient world and familiarize ourselves with its surroundings, a marvelous transformation occurs. We realize that this ancient message, originally addressed to another audience in a distant time and place, speaks powerfully and compellingly to our modern lives. God's ancient word becomes God's modern word for us!

In the following chapters, I have two primary objectives. First, I want to engage in a careful and close reading of the text. The book of Genesis is a literary masterpiece. Not surprisingly, it has been the subject of constant discussion. To some degree, this results from its literary ability to capture our attention and not let us go. The more we read this ancient book, the more difficult it becomes to put it down. However, if we are not careful, we read these familiar texts and make assumptions that may not be present in the texts themselves. We bring our modern ears and eyes to the text, listening and looking for answers that the text may not address, while missing those powerful claims the text intends. Second, I am most interested in articulating the theological riches of this ancient book. Genesis makes powerful affirmations concerning the nature of God, the nature of the world in which we live, the nature of humanity, and the purpose(s) for which we have been created. Genesis is both literary masterpiece and theological masterpiece.

We must mention one final caveat. The biblical writers often assume a body of knowledge that may elude us, since we are not the first audience. Simply put, we tend not to tell listeners those things they already know. The Bible is no exception. Just as we have no need to identify George W. Bush, Al-Qaeda, or explicate the fundamental workings of the Internet in our conversations, so the first recipients of the book of Genesis apparently had no need to identify the Midianites or the Pishon or clarify ancient sheep-breeding practices. Over the past two centuries, archaeological discovery has yielded a wealth of information concerning the world of the ancient Near East (from which the Bible comes). Where appropriate, I will inject information from the larger world of the ancient Near East I think helpful for understanding the message of the biblical text. The ancient Israelites did not live in a vacuum. They lived surrounded by powerful and dominating cultures. Like us, they had to articulate a true vision of God and his will for humanity in a world that held dramatically different opinions about the divine realm and its relation to humanity. Often, I am convinced the theological power of God's word increases as we hear it powerfully proclaimed against the competing and often reigning ideologies of the day.

A Theological Overview of Genesis

To understand Genesis we must first have a sense of the overall framework and movement of the book. Although numerous outlines for the book have been suggested, I have found the theological outline of Walter Brueggemann (*Genesis* in the Interpretation Commentary Series) quite suggestive and valuable for theological reflection.

Scholars all agree that the call of Abraham (Genesis 12:1-3) is the theological center of the book of Genesis. However, Brueggemann uses this motif as a structuring device for the rest of the major blocks of material. Since I find his overall outline suggestive for reading Genesis, I have utilized his larger thematic categories for my reading of Genesis. Genesis 12–25 (the Abraham narrative) he entitles, "The Embraced Call of God," suggesting that the thematic thread that intertwines the various narrative units is the question of Abraham's embracing of God's call or distancing himself from it. The question repeatedly raised is whether Abraham will live by faith. In Genesis 26–36 (the Jacob narrative) the call remains central, but the focus shifts. Here the theme entails "The Conflicted Call of God." The thematic thread that interlaces the various narratives is the conflict that is ever present in the life of Jacob, and the reason(s) for that conflict (i.e., whether the conflict is "self-inflicted" or unavoidable). In Genesis 37–50 (the Joseph narrative) the call of God remains center stage, but again the angle from which it is viewed shifts. In these narratives the promise and presence of God seem strangely "silent." This section Brueggemann entitles, "The Hidden Call of God." Theologically, the issue of providence is at the core of the accounts dealing with Joseph.

Genesis 1–11 remains. Against the backdrop of the patriarchal narratives, Genesis –11 Brueggemann fittingly entitles, "The Sovereign Call of God." Clearly in the opening panoramic sweep of Genesis 1 we see God's clear intent and design for his creation. We are caught up in his purposes for his creation and his understanding of the relationship between himself and his creatures.

However, we are quickly plunged into a series of narratives relating the mixed ways in which his creation (specifically, humanity) responds to these purposes. Throughout the accounts of Adam and Eve, Cain and Abel, Noah and the Flood, and the Tower of Babel, we are invited to interact with "The Sovereign Call of God" and our response to that call. Reading Genesis in this manner ultimately demands that we hear within the Word God's call to us and claim upon our lives, that we see in the lives of Abraham, Jacob, and Joseph our own lives, that in the various responses of God's creatures to his design and intent for his creation, we be challenged to reassess our own (mis)alignment to his will and way for our lives. This is what we mean when we call these materials *Scripture*.

Abraham—Embracing the Call

Viewing the narratives involving Abraham from the perspective of a call/promise embraced opens new vistas for fresh reflection upon familiar passages. Theologically, several of the accounts involving Abraham can be categorized as narratives in which Abraham either embraces the call (faith) or distances himself from the promise (fear). The call and promise to Abraham is introduced in Genesis 12 and reiterated in Genesis 15 and 17. The call rings out:

> *"Go from your country and your kindred and your father's house to the land that I will show you. I will make of you a great nation, and I will bless you, and make your name great, so that you will be a blessing. I will bless those who bless you, and the one who curses you I will curse; and in you all the families of the earth shall be blessed"* (12:1-3).

The Lord's complete commitment to these promises is affirmed in Genesis 15 (where God makes himself totally vulnerable to the promise by moving between the sacrifices); Abraham's acceptance of the promise is invoked in Genesis 17 (through the sign of circumcision indicating commitment to the promise and plan of God). The call of God demands response. Will Abraham embrace this promise, or distance himself from it? Genesis 12–25 is replete with narratives demonstrating the patriarch's willingness to entrust himself to the promise of God. Leaving the security, stability, and community of his homeland, he ventures forth toward an unknown land with a barren wife. Repeatedly Abraham embraces the promise. In this new land we see him willingly erect altars, thereby claiming this land for his God. His confidence in God as provider and promise keeper shines forth in his willingness to allow Lot first choice of this "Promised Land." Later, when Lot (who sees *only* with human eyes) is taken hostage, Abraham unhesitatingly comes to his rescue. However, Abraham refuses any reward for such a deed, eliminating any possible suggestion that he has been enriched by anyone other than his own true God. (A similar motif is present in the purchase of the cave of Machpelah as a burial site for Sarah.) Truly, Abraham as embracer of the promise of God understands the proper relationship between himself and God and thus is deservedly designated as being in "right relationship" (i.e., righteous).

Conversely, the Abraham story reminds us that embracing the call and promise of God is never easy or final. No sooner does Abraham arrive in this "Promised Land" than famine breaks out, forcing his departure. A crisis of faith surfaces; can this God of promise maintain the promise in a foreign land? Unsure, Abraham distances himself from the promise through the duplicitous language he imposes upon Sarah. Strikingly, Abraham, the supposed bearer of the blessings of God, in both instances (i.e., Genesis 12; 20) brings those in contact with him nearer curse than blessing! Further, Abraham, saddled with a barren wife, attempts to "help" God realize the fulfillment of the promise of numerous progeny, first through the proposed adoption of his house servant Eliezer, and then through the birth of Ishmael to Hagar. However, in each instance Abraham is shown that the power of this promising God transcends regional boundaries and human limitations.

Perhaps the focal point at which these themes most clearly and decisively coalesce is in Genesis 22 (the sacrifice of Isaac). Abraham, repeatedly an altar builder, is now asked to build an altar upon which the visible realization of the long-awaited promise will be sacrificed. Surely the promise was never more in jeopardy! Abraham, unflinchingly devoted to the promise and call of his Lord, moves forward, simply yet eloquently expressing for us the heart of the theology under which he now lives his life—"the Lord will provide" (22:8, 14). Abraham in his journey of faith has come to see most clearly that the promising call of God is a sheer manifestation of the gift of a gracious and all-powerful God to whom he can wholeheartedly entrust himself.

Jacob—The Call brings Conflict

When we turn to the narratives involving Jacob we are immediately struck with the element of conflict that permeates the several accounts. Conflict is at the center of Jacob's relationship with Esau (his brother), with Laban (his uncle/father-in-law), and (some would suggest) ultimately with his God. Such a predominance of conflict causes us to question its source and cause. We again are struck with the (perhaps) implicit contrast between Jacob and his forefather Abraham. Whereas Abraham realized that the promise and blessing of God were sheer gifts and received them, Jacob is a *"grasper"* from the outset. At times his grasping even involves deception (thereby fulfilling his name). Although from the outset Esau manifests boorish behavior and a complete disdain for the promises and blessings of God, Jacob refuses to let God's beneficent grace run its course; rather he reaches out and seizes what he so desperately desires. Such grasping and deception force his exodus from the Promised Land, causing us to wonder if the promises of God can once again transcend regional boundaries and human frailties. Poignantly, Jacob's dream at Bethel shows us the promise bearer at a crucial crossroads. The land of promise behind him, the old country of pre-promise before him, Jacob's life is intersected from a third direction—the presence and promise of his God.

Upon arriving in the land of his forebears, Jacob again encounters deception and conflict, although this time apparently not of his own doing. Although Laban unwittingly attempts repeatedly to thwart the plan and purpose of God, we watch God's intent and power to bless and fulfill his promise supersede human machinations. However, a haunting question lingers—will the heir of the promise remain exiled from the land of the promise? Dramatically, difficulties are encountered at both ends of the journey as the promise bearer determines to return home to his father. Having successfully escaped the greedy clutches of his father-in-law, Jacob fearfully anticipates the reception by his estranged brother. Amazingly, upon his arrival Jacob the trickster encounters Esau the brother, a brother who has allowed his animosity to give way to forgiveness and reconciliation.

If the sacrifice of Isaac captures the thematic essence of the Abraham narratives, Jacob's enigmatic wrestling match at the Jabbok may encapsulate the essence of the Jacob narratives. As he nears re-entrance into the Promised Land, Jacob finally becomes acutely aware of the source of his blessings. However, even in this final awakening, Jacob engages in his ultimate struggle—a struggle with God himself. Refusing surrender, Jacob to the end demands both blessing and control through knowledge of his adversary's name. Although the blessing is received, it is in some respects a Pyrrhic victory, for the bearer of the blessing limps home crippled. A man whose life was encircled with conflict is given a new name to reflect such reality—Israel.

The people of Israel surely heard in these ancient narratives of their ancestor Jacob a telling account of their own relationship with God. They could not help but realize the dramatically qualitative difference in a life given to deception and grasping, from a life receptively open to the gracious calling and giving of an all-loving God. Israel, like Jacob before her, had to relearn repeatedly—the stronger the tendency to grasp and force the hand of God, the more prevalent the conflict in one's relationships with others and with God himself.

Joseph—The Hidden Call of God

Viewing the narratives concerning Joseph allows us to see the call from yet a third perspective. It is most striking that God, who has been virtually omnipresent throughout the lives of Abraham and Jacob, suddenly seems absent from the life of Joseph. If we read the adventure of Joseph as if the ending is unknown, the story becomes a catena of potential wrong endings. Joseph, the spoiled child of a doting father, becomes the victim of his brothers' jealousy. However, the pit into which he is thrown fails to become a tomb; rather, he is released only to be sold into Egyptian slavery! Making the best of a bad situation, Joseph rises to a position of responsibility within his master Potiphar's house, only again to be victimized (this time innocently) by the scheming desires of the mistress of the house. Now imprisoned, Joseph makes the best of a miserable situation and rises to a position of responsibility within the prison. Through Joseph's ability to interpret dreams, we are given a glimmer of hope for change in the future; however, we wonder whether his future can really be entrusted to the faulty memory of a royal cupbearer. Again, through the interpretation of dreams, Joseph eventually rises to phenomenal prominence in the land of Egypt, becoming vizier in charge of collection and distribution of food supplies. Again he must confront his brothers, although this time the bases of power from which each party operates is dramatically reversed. Haunting questions refuse to be silenced. Will revenge and retaliation be the order of the day? Where is God in all of this activity? What has happened to the call and promise of God during this period?

Surely two intertwined themes force themselves upon us. On the one hand, the apparent "hiddenness" of God demands attention. Like the reunion of Jacob and Esau, the question of whether revenge or reconciliation will prevail demands resolution. Perhaps the only element more striking than the apparent "absence" of God is a realization of those places where God is mentioned. God occurs regularly on the lips of Joseph, who consistently refuses credit for his ability to interpret dreams. Rather, like Abraham who steadfastly attributes his possessions to an all-giving God, Joseph stresses that his interpretations are solely gifts given him by his God. As we follow the roller coaster ride of Joseph's life, those rare mentions of the presence of God become pivotal to the narrative. The narrator twice informs us of God's presence in Joseph's life—first when he is sold into Potiphar's house and second when he is thrown into the Egyptian prison! Poignantly, precisely when we might (mistakenly) assume that Joseph is bereft of God, God's presence is specifically affirmed!

This theme of the hiddenness (providence) of God leads naturally into the second theme of revenge versus reconciliation. Two passages are of central importance.

> "And now do not be distressed, or angry with yourselves, because you sold me here; for God sent me before you to preserve life. . . . God sent me before you to preserve for you a remnant on earth, and to keep alive for you many survivors. **So it was not you who sent me here, but God;** and he made me a father to Pharaoh, and lord of all his house and ruler over all the land of Egypt" (Genesis 45:5, 7-8).
>
> "Fear not, for am I in the place of God? As for you, **you**

*meant evil against me; but God meant it for good, to bring
it about that many people should be kept alive, as they are today.
So do not fear; I will provide for you and your little ones." Thus
he reassured them and comforted them* (Genesis 50:19-21 RSV,
emphasis added).

In these passages Joseph demonstrates a clear awareness of the presence and purpose of God in his life. Reviewing the former days of
his life, Joseph (with eyes of faith) can see the plan and purpose of
God. Although human forces and machinations may at times seem
formidable and overwhelming, while the plan of God hangs pre-
cariously by the slimmest of threads, Joseph knows that the power
and purpose of his Lord can overcome such seemingly insur-
mountable obstacles. Such is sometimes the life of faith and the
nature of God in our world. When God may seem most absent,
Scripture affirms for us that he is most present. When human caprice
and injustice seem to dominate the landscape, faith enables us to see
clearly the will and way of God in our past, allowing us to embrace
confidently his call and promise as we move into the future.

Genesis—The Sovereign Call of God

Having seen God's gracious provision and beneficent care of
Abraham and his descendants, we are drawn finally to the beginning
of Genesis and driven to ask—what was God's original intent and
purpose for his creation? What was creation's response to this intent?
Will God bring his creation to the unity and purpose he intends?

Genesis 1 opens with a panoramic vision of an undefined mass
that becomes an orderly and purposeful creation solely through
the commanding speech of a Sovereign Lord. God as king issues
directives; a beautiful creation results. Having generated such
majestic beauty with such little effort, this royal monarch rests
enthroned over his creation. Most remarkably, he entrusts his magnificent work to that sole entity of creation fashioned in his own
image—humankind! Created in the image of God, humanity is
bestowed with dignity and responsibility. However, a question
immediately forces itself upon us. How will humankind respond
to this exalted status and bestowal of responsibility?

Genesis 2–11 treats this issue at great length. In Genesis 2, we
are given a vision of God's intent for these humans he has created

and their place and function within the larger created order. In Genesis 3–11 we see humanity's tragic response to this lofty position—rebellion! This all-powerful God has freely given himself to his creation; however, humanity finds itself frequently unable to entrust itself to this loving God. Being created in the image of God is heady stuff—these creatures find that always close at hand is the dangerous temptation to conclude that as humans, they possess or can acquire divine power and ability, making God unnecessary or irrelevant. Time and again we see these creatures strive for equality with God, question God's motivation and intent for their lives, and play God! Such actions are unqualifiedly regarded as rebellion in Genesis 3–11. Not surprisingly, we see that such actions repeatedly plunge God's creation and human society into a whirlpool of tension and struggle for power (Genesis 3), chaos and violence (Genesis 6), and aimlessness and despair (Genesis 11). This God who wills to love and nurture is forced each time to respond with loving punishment. Ultimately rebellion becomes so pervasive that the Sovereign King returns his creation to its pre-created chaotic state, so that he may bring into being a new creation (Genesis 6–9). Tragically, the flood does not drown human desire and hubris, for even in the post-flood world anxiety concerning security and the drive for fame continues (Genesis 11).

However, clearly human rebellion and the attendant divine punishment is not the final word, for we have seen repeatedly that the God of Genesis is a Sovereign Lord who wills in love to call a people into relationship and promises himself totally to that relationship. Appropriately, throughout Genesis 1–11 God returns to renew and reaffirm his commitment to these fickle and shortsighted creatures. Refreshingly, dotting the landscape are individuals who hear the call of this God and respond in obedient trust, acknowledging that this Sovereign God is not only Creator of life and wholeness, but *Sustainer* as well. Such trust results in a relationship with God that is *right*.

Finding Ourselves in Genesis

At the outset of this chapter, I suggested contemporary readers of Genesis typically choose one of two reading strategies. Although many readers assume the ancient text of Genesis can be read through 21st-century eyes with little need for knowledge of the ancient world and worldview, I hope to show that an increased familiarity with the ancient world of Scripture illuminates and clarifies the text of Genesis. This is not to suggest that we *leave* Genesis in the ancient world.

■ Ultimately, our final reading of Genesis must ask—what is God's word in this ancient text for *us* today?
■ How do we hear God's message afresh in our own time and place?

I hope to address such questions in the remaining chapters. For now, a few initial applications will suffice.

Genesis talks much more about *blessing* than salvation. God promises to bless Abraham; Genesis tracks the blessing to Abraham in great detail through the lives of Abraham and his descendants. The promise and call of God have important ramifications for the lives of Abraham and his descendants. Simply put, Abraham and his successors are not brought into special relationship with God so that they might enjoy the benefits of that relationship and hoard the blessings. Rather, Abraham and his descendants are called and blessed for a *purpose*—that they might become a blessing to the rest of God's creation. In an era when Christian (especially evangelical) talk centers almost exclusively on the personal and private benefits of God's saving act in Christ, the message of Genesis provides a powerful reminder that God calls us for a purpose! Put succinctly, the deliverance from sin and salvation God offers us in Jesus Christ is not the *end* of the story, but rather the *beginning*. God's saving act is simply a necessary prerequisite so that we might fulfill God's intent for our lives—to live as agents of blessing. Forgiveness and the bestowal of God's blessings call us, like Abraham, to share those blessings with the rest of humanity.

Genesis is written in such a manner that as we read it we realize we are not simply reading an ancient story, a story of our ancient forebears in the faith. Rather, we are reading *our* story, a narrative written in such a way that we recognize our lives in the lives of Adam and Eve, Cain and Abel, Noah, Abraham, Isaac, Jacob, and Joseph. First and foremost, this is evident by the label we give this material. The book of Genesis falls within the first section of the Bible known in Hebrew as *Torah* (Law). Clearly, *Torah* signifies more than simply *legal dicta* (i.e., rules and regulations). In actuality, the bulk of the Pentateuch (Law) contains much more narrative than legal pronouncements. Recognizing this allows us to redefine our understanding of Law (*Torah*). The books of Genesis through Deuteronomy present us with Law not in our narrow modern sense of legal proscription, but in the larger theological sense of *normative* materials. Against this backdrop, Genesis is normative for us as a story that not only "makes sense" of our own contemporary and individual story, but as a story that places our story within a larger context and connects our story with the great story of God's actions on our behalf. As we engage the narratives of Genesis, we realize that although the historical, cultural, and social settings are dramatically removed from our contemporary setting, the theological contours are strikingly similar. God's call to Abraham to embrace the promise, Abraham's subsequent move between fear and faith, Jacob's grasping that brings conflict to his several relationships, and the apparent hiddenness of God in Joseph's life, resonate with moments in our lives.

While thinking theologically about Genesis may be somewhat daunting and imposing, hearing Genesis theologically is truly dangerous and life threatening. To hear and think theologically about Genesis is to hear God's ancient Word as a word addressed not simply to ancient Israel, but ultimately as a Spirit-breathed Word addressed to us. To hear God's promising call to Abraham is to hear God's promising call to us, a call for us embodied in Jesus Christ. We cannot help but be reminded of those times in which we have faithfully embraced the call of God, or fearfully distanced ourselves from it.

- When specifically have you embraced God's call? How did you move from fear to faith?
- List specific examples in which your struggles with God have resulted in relationship conflicts.
- As with Joseph, when has God seemed "hidden" in your life's circumstances?

To see the conflict in which Jacob's life was embroiled dramatically forces us to consider our lives as anxious graspers or trusting recipients of God's grace. To trace Joseph's life invites us to reexamine our understanding of the hand of God in our own lives, and our need to see life through the eyes of God rather than simply through human eyes. Only with such a vision can reconciliation replace retaliation. As contemporary children of God, hearing God's sovereign call to his creation in Genesis 1–11 permits us to reconsider our place and function as images of God in a world given to rebellion against our loving Creator.

■ Do we truly believe God as Sovereign Lord knows and intends what is best for us as his creatures?
■ Will we willingly align ourselves with this Sovereign King?
■ Will we enter into a relationship with him that he might designate as "righteous?"

Hearing Genesis theologically makes us keenly aware
that such questions cannot be silenced; they demand response.
To hear God's promising call and claim upon his
creation and the ancient patriarchs is ultimately to
hear God's promising call and claim upon us.

To hear and think theologically about Genesis is to hear God's ancient Word as a word addressed not simply to ancient Israel, but ultimately as a Spirit-breathed Word addressed to us. To hear God's promising call to Abraham is to hear God's promising call to us, a call for us embodied in Jesus Christ. We cannot help but be reminded of those times in which we have faithfully embraced the call of God, or fearfully distanced ourselves from it . . . . As contemporary children of God, hearing God's sovereign call to his creation in Genesis 1–11 permits us to reconsider our place and function as images of God in a world given to rebellion against our loving Creator.

CHAPTER 2

In the Beginning
— God (Genesis 1)

n the beginning, when God created the heavens and the earth, the earth was a formless void and darkness covered the face of the deep, while a wind from God swept over the face of the waters. Then God said, "Let there be light"; and there was light.

Genesis opens majestically. The cinematic screen on which the first chapter of the Bible opens spans the universe. As the camera rolls, the theater lights darken. We sit in eerie silence when suddenly the first splash of light bursts forth across the expanse of the screen. The greatest play-write of all time, the Lord of the universe, begins to unveil his masterpiece. Genesis 1 places us squarely in time and space. Temporally, we are at the beginning of the creation; spatially, we have front-row seats in an ancient theater that rivals any modern cinema. We await with eager expectation the opening scene. However, as the opening scene unfolds, we are taken aback, for there is little action. Against this majestic backdrop, there is simply speech! This play involves only one actor, the great Actor of the universe, and he only issues commands!

Yet, what commands those are. God, the majestic Lord of the cosmos, simply speaks and calls his universe and its several parts into being. *"Let there be light . . . and there was light."* In the course of six days God, through simple speech, accomplishes eight creative acts. This first overpowering scene closes as simply as it began. The universe perfectly positioned in time and space, the Sovereign Creator of the universe rests.

Genesis 1 beckons us to address the perennial questions of life. This first scene of Scripture presents us with a world that originates in God and is totally dependent upon that God. It calls us to enter a world called into being and sustained by the gracious power and presence of God. It invites us to think deeply about the relation of the Creator and the creation. It challenges us to enlarge our vision of God's grace, not limiting divine grace solely to the individual, but seeing God's gracious care and compassion in the very warp and woof of the universe! Genesis 1 calls us away from the daily trivialities of our lives to engage the deeper questions. What is the nature of the world in which we live? What is the meaning and purpose of life? What does it mean to be human? Why (for what purpose) were we created? In what or whom does our life find its center?

Creation—A First Look (1:1-2)

In the beginning, when God created the heavens and the earth,
the earth was a formless void and darkness covered the face of
the deep, while a wind from God swept over the face of the waters.

Genesis literally begins, "in the beginning of God's creating . . ." (*bereshit bara' 'elohim*). This opening verse provides the backdrop for all that follows. It captures in one short sentence the essence of the entire first chapter. The scope of Genesis 1 is God's creation of the universe. The optical lens through which we will view these marvelous creative acts of God is a telescope. In these opening verses, we can barely make out the contours of the landscape before us, for darkness casts a pall over everything. Our senses are taxed to the limit. As we peer through the darkness, we become keenly aware of a "formless and normless" mass before us. It has no shape, organization, or seeming purpose. While we wonder at its presence, we faintly hear a breeze moving across this watery mass.

These opening verses of Genesis 1 capture our attention and imagination. They possess everything that demands attentive reading. One of the joys of reading Scripture is that it beckons us to return repeatedly to familiar passages and hear them afresh. The more we read Scripture, the more questions we bring each time to our rereading. As we read these verses, we question anew the relation of the first verse to the second verse. We may read these verses somewhat independently. While verse 1 summarizes the creation of the universe in its essential form, verse 2 focuses our attention upon one aspect of God's creative activity—the earth. Grammatically, we could translate the opening verses of Genesis, *"when God began to create the heavens and the earth, the earth being at that time a formless waste. . . ."* Against this backdrop, God is not simply creating; he is creating order out of chaos (disorder)! The God we worship is a God of order and purpose. God creates with intent; his creation has meaning because of his intent.

We know we have before us a scene of inestimable theological importance. The word chosen to depict God's activity is "create" (*bara'*), a term used only for God. (Elsewhere the text will speak of those things God "makes" [`asah], a term that can be used for either divine or human activity.) References to God's "creating" occur at strategic points in this opening chapter. God "creates" the entire universe (v. 1), the sea monsters (v. 21, masters of the ocean deeps), and humans (v. 27, masters of the land). When God "creates," the "formless void" (literally, "formlessness and normlessness" [*tohu wabohu*]) takes shape and meaning.

Over this watery mass there is movement. Although many readers assume one (and only one) meaning for the Hebrew expression *ruach 'elohim* (i.e., "wind of God" means either "mighty wind" or "spirit [Spirit] of God"), I would suggest the expression is marvelously ambiguous. From one perspective, the image of a powerful (divine) breeze blowing across the face of this disordered watery mass and bringing order to it wonderfully anticipates later Scripture. In Genesis 8:1, God will cause his wind to blow and recede the floodwaters from the earth. In Exodus 14:21, God will send his wind to drive back the waters of the sea so that his people might escape death at the hands of the Egyptians. (In Genesis 3:8, God walks in Eden in the "breezy part" [*ruach*] of the afternoon.) From another perspective, the spirit of God is none other than God himself! Just as the "spirit of a man" is the man himself (see Genesis 45:27; 1 Kings 21:5), so the spirit of God is God himself. If we fast-forward to the exile, we remember Ezekiel's vision of the valley of dry bones (Ezekiel 37). In that unforgettable vision, we see dry (and lifeless) bleached bones littering the valley. As Ezekiel looks across that lifeless wasteland, a breeze begins to move through the valley. The bones come to life, for this is none other than the very breath and spirit of God moving among them! In Genesis 1, we know something powerful and life changing is about to occur, for the very presence of the life-changing spirit of God is moving across the landscape!

The Days of Creation (1:3-25)

Any complexity and ambiguity created by 1:2 quickly gives way to the simplicity and clarity of verses 3-25. Though stunningly beautiful in their presentation, these verses may surprise us with their repetitiveness. The pattern quickly becomes familiar: *"And God said, 'Let there be'... and there was... and God saw that it was good ... and God called... and there was evening and morning, day...."* The structure varies little throughout the days. Each creative day consists of divine command, result, divine approval, and enumeration of the day. The key themes are hard to miss. This divinely created universe is orderly, structured, and the result of divine command. The majesty of the universe results from the spoken word of God across the expanse. Rule and dominion appear throughout. God sits enthroned as Ruler over the entire universe. He commissions the sun, moon, and stars to "rule" the day and night; he entrusts his earthly creation to the rule of humanity (see below).

The orderliness of creation is manifested in the very presentation of the days of creation. From a literary perspective, the arrangement of the days is striking.

Disorder—Incompleteness—"Semi-chaos"	
Separation	**Filling**
DAY #1—Light/Darkness	DAY #4—Sun/Moon/Stars (separation of day/night)
DAY #2—Sky/Water (separation of upper and lower water)	DAY #5—Birds/Fish (to traverse sky and water)
DAY #3—Dry land—Vegetation	DAY #6—Animals/Humans (2 types of plant-eating land-dwellers)
DAY #7—Order—Completeness "God Rested"	

The creation of the universe occurs in parallel panels. Eight acts of creation occur in six days. Days three and six receive a *double dose* of God's creative activity. On the first three days, God separates. On day one, he separates light from darkness. On day two, he separates the upper water from the lower water through the insertion of the sky (firmament) between them. (The imagery for the sky is somewhat akin to that of a colander—the sky is likened to a dome "beaten out" that overarches the waters below and holds back the waters above.) On day three, he surfaces dry land from the waters below, and then populates that dry land with vegetation. Having separated everything into its appropriate compartment, he returns on days four—six to *fill up* those spaces. On day four, he creates "light bearers" (sun, moon, stars) to fill up the light and dark. On day five, he creates fish and birds to inhabit the waters and sky. On day six, he creates land animals and humans to populate the earth. God's creative commanding word results in a universe teeming with life.

Creation is not simply orderly and neatly arranged. It is good! At the close of each day, the Creator surveys his creative act and responds with divine approval. Within the immediate context, the *goodness* of creation is less a moral designation than a functional observation. That is, the diverse elements of creation are "good" in that they correspond appropriately to God's intention. They serve admirably the purpose for which they were created! Put differently, the orderliness and predictability of the universe is *not* due to a series of indifferent and impersonal "laws of nature," but to the faithful participation of a loving Creator who wills to sustain his creation. When read against the backdrop of the larger ancient Near East, this simple declaration of the goodness of God's creative acts takes on added meaning. First, Genesis 1 decisively affirms that creation stands subordinate to and dependent upon God. Even the heavenly bodies are not independent of God, but stand in his service (designating the seasons and separating day and night). The earth produces vegetation; the animals stand at God's disposition. Second, in contrast to her neighbors who deified various elements of the created order (e.g., astral phenomena), the Bible resolutely declares that all the created elements are the result of God's creative touch and refuses to substitute worship of the Creator for the creature. Paul captures eloquently the tragedy when Genesis 1 is distorted—worship of the Creator is jettisoned for worship of the creature (Romans 1:18-23). Perverse religion offers worship to something that was intended itself to offer worship!

Created in the Image of God (1:26-31)

Then God said, "Let us make humankind in our image, according to our likeness; and let them have dominion over the fish of the sea, and over the birds of the air, and over the cattle, and over all the wild animals of the earth, and over every creeping thing that creeps upon the earth."

So God created humankind in his image, in the image of God he created them; male and female he created them.

> *God blessed them, and God said to them, "Be fruitful and multiply, and fill the earth and subdue it; and have dominion over the fish of the sea and over the birds of the air and over every living thing that moves upon the earth."*

With this declaration we reach the apex of creation. The staccato repetition of the earlier days of creation gives way to a detailed rendering of the creation of humanity. The scene begins with God verbalizing his intent to create human beings in his image. It next transcribes God's sole dialogue with his created order—he commands directly these humans he has created to fill the earth and take control. It concludes with his affirmation that his creation is "very good" (envisioning either the creation of *humanity* or the *entirety* of creation).

This passage fascinates us, for it bristles with unanswered questions and carries heavy theological freight. We cannot help but wonder to whom God is speaking (v. 26). We long to determine exactly the nature and essence of being in the image of God. We live in a world fascinated with divine blessing; here humankind is blessed and commissioned. To each of these issues we must attend.

When read through the eyes of later Christian interpretation and theological thought, the answer to the first issue seems self-evident. A popular interpretation of Genesis 1:26 finds in the line "let us make humankind in our image" a stunning reference to the Trinity. Such an interpretation ignores the question of whether such a reference would be relevant or comprehensible to the original audience. It assumes Scripture speaks primarily and principally to later generations of believers. When read against its ancient backdrop, I would suggest other readings become more compelling. The text assumes the ancient world both in imagery and in language. First, the imagery envisions God surrounded by his divine council. The image of God as omnipotent monarch seated on a throne and surrounded by divine beings runs throughout the Old Testament (see 1 Kings 22; Psalm 82; Job 1–2; Isaiah 6). The picture of God as sovereign monarch dominates the theological landscape of Genesis 1. Not surprisingly, the divine speech matches the imagery. We label the use of a plural pronoun ("let us") by a single speaker the "royal we" or "plural of majesty." The ancient Near East provides ample evidence of royalty speaking in the plural. Although the king says "we," the royal council knows its task will be to execute faithfully the directives of the monarch. Remarkably, the God we worship chooses not to remain alone in his universe, but to create a sector of his universe with which he will have dialogue and fellowship.

This leads to our second question. What does it mean to be created in the image (*tselem*) of God? Determining the answer is difficult, for we want most to know the *essence* of the image, while the text desires to tell us the *function* of that image. While speculation abounds regarding the correct interpretation of the essence of the image of God, the functional significance of the image of God seems clear. Created in the image of God means we have dominion over God's earthly creation. Just as God has ultimate responsibility for the entirety of his universe, so he has given humankind responsibility for the earthly domain. Amazingly, he has entrusted the earth to us!

Again, reading this section of Scripture against its original ancient Near Eastern setting provides insight. In the ancient Near East, when kings marched forth to bring outlying provinces into their orbit of control, they often would erect a statue of themselves in the conquered territory before departing for their homeland. This symbolic act was striking. As the conquered peoples went to and fro in their daily activities, they were constantly reminded of their controlling overlord as they passed the "image" (*tselem*) of the reigning monarch. (In a slightly different vein, an inscription of Ramses II on the Syrian coast reads, "the Pharaoh is the living image of the gods on earth.") In Genesis 1, God chooses to "image" himself in humankind! The theological vision is powerful—God, the supreme sovereign of the universe, bestows royalty upon his created subjects. They receive exalted status—only they bear the image, only they receive direct communication. Although the larger context is clearly monarchical, the language is "democratized." *All* humans, *male and female*, are created in the image of God. In contrast to the ancient Near East, where *images* are typically limited to royal figures, God's image carries no socio-economic, ethnic, or gender distinctions.

The imagery is breathtaking. Created in the image of the reigning monarch of the universe clearly implies that humans are vice-regents ("princes and princesses")! Such a metaphor is heady stuff, especially when coupled with the language of rule and dominion. However, before we overdose on power, we must remember the vision of "rule/dominion" given us by God. Consistently throughout the Old Testament, God demonstrates genuine rulership. To "subdue" the earth does *not* carry negative connotations of a despotic tyrant devastating the countryside, but envisions dominion as reflected in God's own treatment of his creation. The images that dominate God's rulership are that of a shepherd tending sheep or a parent caring for a child. In the Old Testament, the king was entrusted with the care and welfare of his people; he exercised his dominion through the bestowal of blessing upon the land. Psalm 72 beautifully captures the sense of rule:

> *Give the king your justice, O God,*
> *and your righteousness to a king's son.*
> *May he judge your people with righteousness,*
> *and your poor with justice. . . .*
> *May he defend the cause of the poor of the people,*
> *give deliverance to the needy, and crush the oppressor. . . .*
> *May he be like rain that falls on the mown grass,*
> *like showers that water the earth.*
> *In his days may righteousness flourish*
> *and peace abound, until the moon is no more.*
> *May he have dominion from sea to sea,*
> *and from the River to the ends of the earth* (vv. 1-2,4,6-8).

Sabbath Rest (2:1-3)

Having created the entire universe in six dramatic movements, God rests on day seven. At first blush, day seven may surprise us. We cannot help but ask, is God tired? Does God really get tired? Or, to put it somewhat tongue in cheek, how can God be tired after six days of simply speaking? We clearly recognize that more than meets the eye must be present, for this is the only day of the week that is *blessed* and *made holy*. The Sabbath receives significant treatment in the Old Testament and can be read profitably from a variety of angles. At this stage, I will simply suggest *one* possible lens through which we might view this final scene in the opening drama of creation. As mentioned above, when ancient Near Eastern kings marched forth and took control of surrounding territories, they often would erect a statue (image) of themselves before their departure to remind the subject peoples of their power and presence. Similarly, these royal figures would also often commission inscriptions to be penned commemorating their control. A favorite royal idiom of these inscriptions, used to declare the monarch's complete control, was, "I *rested* over that city/province/country." In like manner, one possible reading of day seven envisions the Sovereign Lord of the universe declaring his supreme control and mastery of his created universe—the Lord *rested*. The implications of such a vision are powerful. From this vantage point, every seven days God's people were called to cease their *normal* labors so that they might remind themselves and the surrounding nations that the world was safely in the hands of their all-powerful God and Sovereign Lord of the universe. The God who had created this marvelous world would not let his creation self-destruct. Appropriately, this *blessed* and *holy* day uniquely completed the week.

Genesis 1 and the World of the Ancient Near East

I have noted several points at which I believe a knowledge of the world of the ancient Near East provides helpful insights into the biblical text. God's people did not live in a vacuum, nor did his word go forth free from context. Rather, ancient Israel lived surrounded by nations with powerful narratives about the origins of the world and the people in it. We have creation texts from Egypt to Mesopotamia. These narratives document in detail how Israel's neighbors understood the world and its origins, the divine realm, and their relation to that divine realm.

Perhaps the document most relevant for dialogue with Genesis 1 is a Babylonian account of creation entitled *Enuma Elish* ("when on high"). *Enuma Elish* is simply *one* Babylonian account of creation. In reality, unlike Genesis 1, its primary purpose is not to detail the origins of the universe, but to tell how the chief god of Babylon, Marduk, became the chief god of the universe, and to *celebrate* his supremacy. To understand *Enuma Elish* (and any other ancient Near Eastern text from Egypt, Canaan, or Mesopotamia), we must remember that these ancient peoples assumed the universe was heavily populated with gods and goddesses, just as the earth was heavily populated with humans. These texts attempt to explain, to one degree or another, why the earth and humanity are the way they are.

As *Enuma Elish* opens, nothing is present except the great divine parents—Apsu (freshwater) and Tiamat (saltwater), and their son Mummu (mist?). (The story travels a significant distance before we arrive at creation.) These three commingle to form an immense, undefined mass from which the later universe will be made. Apsu and Tiamat soon give birth to children who beget children. Soon gods and goddesses are everywhere. Trouble soon erupts. The younger gods party vigorously, creating a level of noise that deprives the older Apsu of his sleep. Desperate, Apsu determines to destroy the noisemakers. He declares, "I'll destroy them . . . that silence may be established . . . and we may sleep." When the news of this plan reaches the younger gods, they are filled with consternation. They roam aimlessly. However, one of their number, Ea (alternately Enki), the god of wisdom, devises a plan. As the god of magic, he encircles the gods with a protective ring and composes an incantation that puts Apsu to sleep! While asleep, Ea removes the royal crown from Apsu's head, slays him, and imprisons Mummu. (Tiamat is left unmolested, since she apparently had little sympathy with Apsu's plan.)

Life returns to normal. The parties return as robust as ever; Ea marries Damkina and builds a palace over the slain Apsu. Unfortunately, the widow Tiamat now becomes the restless wanderer. As she roams about aimlessly, she is joined by Kingu (a ringleader of the evil gods). Kingu convinces Tiamat she must avenge the death of Apsu (to maintain respect). Tiamat marries Kingu, gives him dominion over the rest of the gods, and determines to wage war against her slain husband's assailants. When the news breaks of Tiamat's plan, the despair of the gods is greater than before. Even Ea seems intimidated. However, during the time lapse, Ea and Damkina have birthed an impressive young god— Marduk. Although considerably younger than the other gods, Marduk is enlisted to fight Tiamat. He agrees, on the condition that with his victory he will become king of the gods! The agreement sealed, Marduk prepares his weapons.

The mere appearance of Marduk throws Kingu and his cohorts into confusion. Like true bullies, they tuck tail and flee. Tiamat, however, is unflappable. She extends a friendly greeting to Marduk, but when he denounces her plan, she quickly spins into a frenzy. She opens her mouth to devour Marduk; however, he drives an evil wind down her throat, distending her body and distracting her. He then captures her with his net and shoots an arrow into her open mouth. It strikes her heart, killing her. The remaining evil gods are captured and imprisoned.

Marduk becomes king of the universe and the parties resume. *Finally* we arrive at the creation of the universe! Marduk slices the colossal body of Tiamat in half and fashions the universe (half sky; half earth). As king of the gods, he commissions the various gods to tasks and stations in that universe. He establishes the constellations and fixes the calendar. Importantly, he makes the imprisoned gods servants to the victors. Their menial tasks are burdensome. They soon ask for relief. Sympathetic, Marduk addresses their plight. He kills Kingu and mixes his blood with the dust of the earth. Out of this mixture he fashions humanity! These newly created humans are now entrusted with the menial work of the formerly imprisoned gods. Humans will now provide for the needs of the gods and goddesses, so that they might live lives of leisure (lives appropriate for deities).

A first encounter with *Enuma Elish* may leave the reader thoroughly confounded. Near Eastern mythology takes us into a world (and worldview) markedly different from our modern scientific world. However, it was a world fully known to the patriarchs and their ancestors. It was a world with which they likely interacted at crucial moments in their history. It was a world at odds with their God and his revelation of himself and his will. In a world sometimes dominated by these ancient narratives, the people of God faithfully proclaimed the true God, the true narrative of the beginnings of the universe, and the true vision of what it meant to live in right relationship with the sole Creator and Sustainer of the universe.

Of what value for us are these ancient Near Eastern tales? First, we must remember that we are not talking of *borrowing*. *Enuma Elish* is neither the sole Mesopotamian account of the origins of the universe, nor the authoritative account. Rather, the value of *Enuma Elish* is that it reminds us of how differently Scripture presents God, the world, and humanity in comparison to the surrounding cultures. It highlights for us the theological power of the biblical account.

A few examples will suffice. First, in contrast to the Babylonian worldview, Genesis 1 reminds us that creation is simply that—creation! The created elements of the universe are not deities to be worshiped or feared. (Paul affirms the same in Colossians.) Second, creation does not result from conflict, since there is no divine being in the universe competent to challenge the all-powerful Lord of creation. Our God's awesome command of creation is doubly heightened—he is so powerful he simply *speaks* and the world comes into being! Third, and perhaps most strikingly, humans are neither an afterthought nor mere lackeys for the divine realm. Rather, they are creatures invested with dignity, worth, and *responsibility*. In the image of their divine Creator, they are charged with the incredible task of caring for the earth their Sovereign Lord has created. Finally, in answer to the perennial question whether humans are good or bad, we receive a resounding response. Whereas in Mesopotamia humanity is likely prone to evil, given the blood of Kingu in their genetic makeup, Scripture reminds us that we are created in the image of God and declared *good* by this same Creator. In an ancient world politically and militarily dominated by the countries surrounding Israel, the people of God returned repeatedly to this ancient narrative of creation to affirm God's sovereign rulership of the world. Regardless of the daily circumstances that might occur, Genesis 1 resolutely reminded them that they could live with confidence, for their God *rested* over his creation.

Finding Ourselves in Genesis 1

Genesis 1 has been frequently read and much discussed in Christian circles. It has often been the subject of heated debates centering on the relationship of the Bible and Science. However, an arena where Genesis 1 has often been most glaringly absent in Christian circles is the very arena in which it figures so prominently in Scripture—worship! In ancient Israel, creation was a topic central to worship. The ancient Israelites read Genesis 1 and broke into joyous and worshipful celebration. Creation turns up prominently in the Psalms, ancient Israel's hymnbook. Simply put, Genesis 1 put to music appears in Psalm 8:

> O LORD, *our Sovereign,*
> *how majestic is your name in all the earth!*
> *You have set your glory above the heavens.*
> *Out of the mouths of babes and infants*

you have founded a bulwark because of your foes,
to silence the enemy and the avenger.
When I look at your heavens, the work of your fingers,
the moon and the stars that you have established;
what are human beings that you are mindful of them,
mortals that you care for them?
Yet you have made them a little lower than God,
and crowned them with glory and honor.
You have given them dominion over the works of your hands;
you have put all things under their feet,
all sheep and oxen,
and also the beasts of the field,
the birds of the air, and the fish of the sea,
whatever passes along the paths of the seas.
O LORD, *our Sovereign,*
how majestic is your name in all the earth!

The psalmist lifts our eyes and spirits to the heavens. He marvels at the awesome creative power of God manifested in the expansiveness and intricacy of the universe. The psalmist reminds us that in worship, creation is less a phenomenon to be analyzed systematically and more a living masterpiece to be celebrated and lauded. Hearing Genesis 1 in Psalm 8 carries theological overtones. It calls us to self-examination.

■ As we read Genesis 1, do we envision more the recitation of an atomic chart, or a virtuoso performance by a stellar symphony?

More specifically, Psalm 8 reminds us of two most important theological truths. First, the proper response when hearing we are created in the image of God is to acknowledge humble consternation! The psalmist reminds us that our creation in God's image says less about us and more about the marvelous grace of the God we worship. To paraphrase his central line, we humbly exclaim,

"When I look at all the marvelous elements in your glorious creation, I wonder, 'why did you designate humans as your crowning achievement?'" How is this true for you?

Second, the structure of the psalm reminds us of our proper place in creation. The divine Lord of the universe created us to live in relationship with him. However, created in the image of God carries the dangerous temptation to think more highly of ourselves than we ought.

■ Why is it true that the only way to remain truly humble is to remind ourselves that as God's created image we are surrounded by God himself?

The psalm begins and ends with
"O LORD, our Sovereign, how majestic is your name in all the earth!"

Creation figures prominently in other psalms. In Psalm 19, creation and the law join hands and hearts to praise God.

> *The heavens are telling the glory of God;*
> *and the firmament proclaims his handiwork.*
> *Day to day pours forth speech,*
> *and night to night declares knowledge.*
> *There is no speech, nor are there words;*
> *their voice is not heard;*
> *yet their voice goes out through all the earth,*
> *and their words to the end of the world* (vv. 1-4).

In the remainder of that psalm, the psalmist declares that God receives praise from two crucial sectors of his creation—while the inanimate heavens and earth proclaim God's glory *without words*, God's animated creatures, human beings, declare praise to God through their *keeping of his spoken word* (the Law). We are the only element of God's creation through whom praise becomes articulate. Strikingly, both God's creation and his law are a result of his commanding speech!

Creation figures prominently in ancient Israelite worship; it challenges us to incorporate it more fully into our contemporary worship. Clearly Genesis 1 reminds us of the great theological truths we hold so dear. It calls us to celebrate that we live in a world that originated with God and is dependent upon him for life. It reminds us that the relation of the Creator and his creation is not one of domineering master and servile subject, but faithful commitment and gracious invitation. It calls us to remember that

God's grace is larger than the individual—it operates and moves throughout the entire created order. In Genesis 1 we see the marvelous interplay between God's awe-inspiring transcendence and his loving immanence. The God we worship simultaneously sits enthroned in the heavens and engages in conversation with his creation. Having seen God in Genesis 1, we are not completely surprised when he later manifests his sovereign power in the form of a servant through his Son Jesus.

Genesis 1 keeps those deepest questions squarely before us.

■ What is the nature of the world in which we live?
■ What is the meaning and purpose of life?
■ What does it mean to be human? Why (for what purpose) were we created?
■ In what/whom does our life find its center?

To these questions Genesis 1 resoundingly responds—we are creatures of dignity and worth, for we have been created in the image of God. Our lives have meaning and purpose, for God has created us and given us responsibility. Genesis 1 provides us a powerful paradox. On the one hand, we find in Genesis 1 an incomparable Creator, a Creator who calls into being galaxies and constellations with a simple word. On the other hand, this incomparable Creator has chosen to reflect himself in one element of his creation—us! Created in God's image, we are created for relationship with him. Creation implies belonging to God. God has freely chosen to image himself not in one form, but in two—male and female. It is *humankind* that is created in the image of God. Through God's inexplicable graciousness, we become the "great exception" in his universe.

Gift carries responsibility. To paraphrase Jesus, "to whom much is given, much is required" (Luke 12:48). Created in the image of God, we affirm that we are not mere matter, but divine representatives. In the ancient world, Israel stood somewhat unique. Surrounded by nations sporting idols and images, Israel lived aniconic (without idols). Throughout the Old Testament, Israel was forbidden to construct or erect idols. Although several reasons are given in the Old Testament, two seem appropriate in the context of Genesis 1. First, an idol is an attempt to capture the stature and grandeur of the god(dess) it represents (through the size and value of the materials used). At this point Israel is stymied, since everything in the created order pales in comparison to the Creator who made those elements!

> *To whom then will you compare me,*
>> *or who is my equal? says the Holy One.*
> *Lift up your eyes on high and see:*
> **Who created these?**
> *He who brings out their host and numbers them,*
>> *calling them by name;*
>> *because he is great in strength,*
>> *mighty in power,*
>> *not one is missing* (Isaiah 40: 25-26, emphasis added).

Second, there is no need for us to construct an image of God, for God has already made one of himself—us! We *stand before God*, and move throughout his world, as *living images*. Herein lies the rub. An image of wood or stone stays put and "behaves itself." God chooses the more risky path of imaging himself in flesh and blood. The question just below the surface at the close of Genesis 1 is whether this "image" will faithfully reflect the Creator.

As children of God, we know the tragic answer to that question. The subsequent history of God's "images" testifies to the loss of theological vision provided by Psalm 8 and the ambitious and repeated attempts by the image to dethrone the Image-Maker! The irony is rich—that *one* sector of creation (humanity) God declared his crowning achievement often fails to offer praise and instead engages in repeated attempts to dethrone the Sovereign Lord of the universe and enthrone itself.

■ In what ways have you dethroned God in your life? List specific times when you have exchanged praising God for seeking praise for yourself.

As Christians, we acknowledge God's ultimate response to this arrogant endeavor to dethrone him. God manifests his image quintessentially in his own Son—Jesus Christ (Colossians 1:15; Philippians 2:6; Hebrews 1:3; John 1:14,18). In the life of Jesus we find the epitome of the divine image. In Jesus of Nazareth all the themes of Genesis 1 come together.

> *He is the image of the invisible God, the firstborn of all creation; for in him all things in heaven and on earth were created, things visible and invisible, whether thrones or dominions or rulers or powers—all things have been created through him and for him. He himself is before all things, and in him all things hold together. He is the head of the body, the church; he is the beginning, the firstborn from the dead, so that he might come to have first place in everything. For in him all the fullness of God was pleased to dwell, and through him God was pleased to reconcile to himself all things, whether on earth or in heaven, by making peace through the blood of his cross* (Colossians 1:15-20).

> *In the beginning was the Word, and the Word was with God, and the Word was God. He was in the beginning with God. All things came into being through him, and without him not one thing came into being. What has come into being in him was life, and the life was the light of all people. The light shines in the darkness, and the darkness did not overcome it. . . . And the Word became flesh and lived among us, and we have seen his glory, the glory as of a father's only son, full of grace and truth* (John 1:1-5,14).

In Jesus the creative and all-powerful Word of God becomes enfleshed. In Jesus we see the brilliant light dispelling the darkness so that the beauty of God's creation can shine forth clearly. In Jesus we see God's image reflected most perfectly as the image points faithfully to the Image-Maker.

We can do no better than join with Paul in celebrating in wonder at this marvelous gift God has bestowed upon us.

> *Let the same mind be in you that was in Christ Jesus,*
> *who, though he was in the form of God,*
> *did not regard equality with God*
> *as something to be exploited,*
> *but emptied himself,*
> *taking the form of a slave,*
> *being born in human likeness.*

And being found in human form,
he humbled himself
and became obedient to the point of death—
even death on a cross.
Therefore God also highly exalted him
and gave him the name
that is above every name,
so that at the name of Jesus every knee should bend,
in heaven and on earth and under the earth,
and every tongue should confess
that Jesus Christ is Lord,
to the glory of God the Father (Philippians 2:5-11).

In Jesus the creative and all-powerful Word of God becomes enfleshed. In Jesus we see the brilliant light dispelling the darkness so that the beauty of God's creation can shine forth clearly. In Jesus we see God's image reflected most perfectly as the image points faithfully to the Image-Maker.

CHAPTER 3

In the Beginning—
Male & Female

(Genesis 2–3)

enesis 2–3 revisits creation, but the thoroughly theocentric (God-centered) view of creation gives way to the anthropocentric (human-centered) aspect of that created order. Where Genesis 1 calls us to look through the telescope and so we initially are struck by the watery expanse of our world, Genesis 2 calls us to observe creation through a microscope. As we focus on one particular sector of God's created world, we see before us an arid desert. As that vision comes clearly into focus, we see God planting a garden in the midst of that dry expanse.

Genesis 2–3 must be read as a single unit. It consists of three major scenes: Adam and Eve in the garden (2:7-25); the temptation (3:1-7); the punishment of Adam and Eve (3:8-24). Four major characters dominate the landscape: God, Adam, Eve, and the serpent. The contrast between chapters two and three is striking. The garden is given and then lost; the first couple comes to full life, and then watches that life disintegrate through disobedience. Key phrases occur at the opening (2:4-9,15) and closing (3:22-24) of the narrative.

Genesis 2–3 manifests a favorite literary style of the biblical writers. The literary artistry of these two chapters is exquisite. We call this style *ring composition*. Simply put, the story is written in such a way that invites readers to "back out" in reverse order from the way they enter. In chapter two, the movement is as follows: creation of man > place for man > companionship for man > creation of woman. Chapter three reverses chapter two. The outline (Outline 1) on page 44 captures this literary artistry.

Like Genesis 1, these chapters address the most fundamental issues of our lives. Who is God? What does it mean to be human? What is the nature of the divine—human relationship? Why is our world the way it is? Before addressing these questions, it is appropriate that we again acknowledge our preconceptions concerning this text. For many readers of the Bible, these chapters are considered the definitive text for all that follows (hence language of "the Fall"). For many this is the definitive text addressing the origins of evil in our world. For others this explains the origin of death in our

---

OUTLINE 1 ■

(A) "These are the generations . . ." (2:4)

  (B) The field is unworked—there is no one to till ground (2:5-6)

    (C) A human being is given life and installed in the Garden (2:7-17)

      (D) The man prefers human companionship over beasts (2:18-22)

        (E) The man calls his companion "woman" (2:23)

          (F) Summary—"therefore a man leaves . . ." (2:24)

            (G) The human couple is "naked and not ashamed" (2:25)

              (H) A serpent promises—"eyes will be opened" (3:1-5)

                (I) Transgression (3:6)

              (H) The couple's "eyes are opened" (3:7a)

            (G) The couple experiences shame (3:7b-10)

          (F) Summary—"for you are dust" (3:19b)

        (E) The man calls his companion "Eve" (life-bearer) (3:20)

      (D) The man and woman wear skins of beasts (3:21)

    (C) Humans are expelled from the Garden and denied immortality (3:22-24)

  (B) Field work begins (3:23b)

(A) The birth of a child completes one generation (4:1)

---

world. Still others see the principal (and perhaps overwhelming) issue the subject of sex and the evils it brings. Although all of these perspectives may capture a crucial aspect of the text, I would suggest that focusing upon one perspective to the exclusion of others diminishes the theological richness of the text. I would suggest that Genesis 2–3 call us to reflect upon the purposes of God in our world and the ability/inability of humanity to trust in those purposes. Genesis 2–3 provides us a vision of God, a vision of humankind, and a vision of the world in which we live.

In Genesis 1, God is preeminently pictured as a royal monarch enthroned above his universe. He speaks in commanding tones and creates effortlessly. In Genesis 2–3, God appears in multiple roles. He is gardener (planter), builder, and (perhaps) preeminently potter/sculptor. Elsewhere in Scripture God as Potter expresses his sovereignty (see Isaiah 29:15-16; 45:9-13; Jeremiah 18:1-6; Roman 9:20-21).

God is fully and intimately engaged in his created world. Because of that, the vision of humankind in Genesis 2–3 is relational. Throughout humans are presented in their various relationships. Humans have relationships with the earth and its created elements, with each other (male/female), and with God. In Genesis 1, meaningful life results because we are created in God's image. In Genesis 2, God gives his first human creature meaningful life through three dimensions: vocation (v. 15—Adam is to "work the garden"); permission (v. 16—Adam has free run of the garden); prohibition (v. 17—Adam is not to eat of the tree of knowledge of good and evil). We dare not miss these dimensions of meaningful life. Rarely, if ever, do we as humans ponder why God gave Adam incredible permission in the garden! Rather, we obsess over why God would plant a tree in the garden and then deny his creature access to that tree! From another angle, Genesis 2 affirms that one aspect of God's creation that brings meaning to our lives is vocation—what we do. God's original intent for us is that our lives have purpose and we find meaning through what we do. Just as Genesis 1 calls us to reflect seriously on the place of time (Sabbath) in our lives, so Genesis 2 calls us to reflect seriously on the place of work in our lives.

At this point we can make several large comparisons between the vision of creation portrayed in Genesis 1 and that depicted in Genesis 2–3. Although of one piece theologically, they express that theological vision from different vistas. Just as the four gospels give us four wonderful portraits of Jesus, so Genesis 1 and 2 give us two wonderful vantage points from which to view God's creative feats.

Genesis 1	Genesis 2–3
"Telescopic"	"Microscopic"
Order/Formulaic	Story
"Good"	Harmony/Unity
Speech = Command	Speech = Dialogue
"Big Picture"	Focus on Humanity
God = Monarch	God = Sculptor/Gardener/Builder
Humanity = Royal	Humanity = Relational

Life in the Garden (2:4-25)

The scene opens simply, yet eloquently. In the midst of an expansive desert, God plants a beautiful and well-watered garden. That garden is home to a host of marvelous plants and trees. They are not only beautiful, they are functional—they are "good for food." This garden is truly a delightful pleasure (Hebrew—*eden*). In this garden God locates his first human creation—Adam. The name is appropriate. Since he was created from the earth (*adamah*), he is named *Adam* ("earthling"). This *Adam* exhibits both frailty (dust) and empowerment (inbreathed by God). In Genesis 1, humans are unique in that only they receive direct speech from God; in Genesis 2, humans are unique in that only they are infused with the very breath of God. (The old notion that humans are unique in that only they have a soul is based on a mistranslation in the KJV. Both animals and humans have a "soul" [*nephesh*].)

As we noted earlier, human life finds meaning through vocation (work). However, we soon discover that vocation alone cannot provide complete meaning. Adam lacks companionship. The Creator God provides Adam animals and entrusts them to his care. Adam gives them identity through naming. Whereas in Genesis 1 human control over the rest of creation is expressed through the language of image, rule, and dominion, in Genesis 2 it is expressed through the language of naming. However, when the naming of the animals is completed, no animal fully matches Adam.

The language is striking, and worthy of fuller comment.

> "The man gave names to all cattle, and to the birds of the air, and to every living animal of the field; but for the man there was not found **a helper as his partner** (`ezer kenegdo)" (2:20, emphasis added).

To address this situation, God puts Adam into a deep sleep, performs surgery, and constructs a fitting counterpart to his first creature. When Adam awakes, he exclaims, "Wow, now this is what I had in mind!" (a somewhat loose, but accurate paraphrase). The scene is riveting; the language is dramatic. Whereas Adam originated out of the clay of the earth, his counterpart originates from his rib. The man functions for the creation of the woman as the earth did for the creation of the man. Unlike the animals, she realizes fully God's provision for the man as a "fit helper."

Although numerous readers of this narrative assume the term "helper" denotes inferiority or subordination, such an assumption is highly questionable. Elsewhere in the Old Testament, this term is used in relationships suggesting inferiority/superiority, equality, or superiority/inferiority. In the Psalms, a favorite designation used for God is "helper" (see Psalms 33:20; 70:5; 115:9-11; 121:1-2; 124:8; 146:4; cf. also Exodus 18:4; Deuteronomy 33:7,26). Surely no one would suggest God functions as an inferior when helping humans! The key to determining the *nature* of the relationship lies in the accompanying qualifier—"as his partner" (*kenegdo*). Literally, this term means "corresponding to him." (Elsewhere in Scripture this term designates a relationship of equality and correspondence.)

Taking the text at face value, we assume the relationship is based on equality. Such a view fits the larger context nicely. From a theological perspective, Genesis 2 presents Adam in three relationships. He has a relationship with God, a relationship with the animal realm, and a relationship with woman. In his relationship with God, the posture is that of inferior (Adam)—Superior (God). In his relationship with the animals, the posture is that of superior (Adam)—inferior (animals). In his relationship with woman, the posture is that of equality.

Some might suggest that the man—woman relationship is that of superior—inferior, since Adam names the woman, like the animals. However, a close reading of the text shows that the grammatical construction *changes* between the two namings. When Adam names the animals, the grammatical construction reflects the traditional construction of defining, ordering, and controlling. When Adam names the woman, the grammatical construction changes and the element of exclamation appears. Interestingly, as he excitedly "names" this creature "woman" (*ishshah*), he simultaneously names himself "man" (*ish*)!

> *Then the man said,*
> *"This at last is bone of my bones*
> *and flesh of my flesh;*
> *this one shall be called Woman,*
> *for out of Man this one was taken."*
> *Therefore a man leaves his father and his mother and clings to his*
> *wife, and they become one flesh* (Genesis 2:23-24).

It is worthy of note that the text envisions the man leaving his family to join his wife; later social customs typically reflected a practice in which the woman left her family to join her husband's family. More importantly, the language is covenant language. Adam's initial observation (and assessment) of the woman focuses entirely upon their commonality and mutuality. Remarkably, the one (alone) Adam, no sooner having become two, finds oneness in a mutual relationship. Earlier God gave Adam a *vocation* to bring meaning, now he gives Adam a *companion* to bring joy. Life in the garden begins with the creation of man, it concludes with the creation of woman.

The Garden in Jeopardy (3:1-7)

The closing of chapter 2 and opening of chapter 3 are linked through wordplay:

> *And the man and his wife were both naked ['arummim], and were not ashamed. Now the serpent was more crafty ['arum] than any other wild animal that the LORD God had made* (Genesis 2:25–3:1).

The precise import of this comment is left ambiguous at this stage. We cannot help but wonder whether this opening statement intends a contrast between the wise craftiness of the serpent and the naïve innocence of the human couple.

The brief dialogue between the serpent and the human couple is poignant and filled with dramatic irony. The serpent opens with a seemingly innocent question, only to follow the woman's reply with a direct challenge to God's truthfulness! According to the serpent, God is not playing straight with these creatures to whom he has seemingly entrusted so much. Rather, he is engaging in self-protection to insure these creatures do not become like him. Made (`asah) by God, this most cunning representative of the animal kingdom threatens the harmony of the created order and challenges the intent of the Creator. What God presents as a *given*, the serpent presents as an *option*. (Interestingly, for the first time in Scripture, God appears in the third person. The serpent is the first to make him an *object* of discussion.)

The woman's response is also telling. In actuality, the first interpreter of the divine word is the woman. She demonstrates a hermeneutical method that later rabbis will revere. She hedges the divine word! She responds that not only may they not *eat* of the fruit of the tree of knowledge of good and evil, they may not even *touch* it! In actuality, Eve interprets a command for which she was not present! If we simply read the text as it stands (without importing at this stage other biblical texts treating Adam and Eve), the woman seems intelligent, informed, and perceptive. She assumes responsibility for obedience to a command delivered originally to the man (a responsibility the man will quickly abdicate—3:12). No reason is given for the serpent's selection of the woman, and so speculation abounds.

A popular rendering of this story envisions Eve taking the fruit, eating, and then going in search of Adam to share the pleasures of the fruit with him. The text reads:

> So when the woman saw that the tree was good for food, and that it was a delight to the eyes, and that the tree was to be desired to make one wise, she took of its fruit and ate; and she also gave some to her husband, **who was with her**, and he ate (3:6, emphasis added).

Elsewhere in the Old Testament where the phrase "who was with" occurs, the accompanying party has been present from the beginning! (It is worthy of note that the serpent consistently addresses the woman with the plural and she answers with the plural.) We should probably similarly assume that Adam has been present (and strangely silent) throughout this whole conversation! He will soon become verbose!

The brevity of this scene does not do justice to its theological importance. This scene provides us with our first encounter of the nature of sin. Simply put, sin is rebellion. Sin is essentially questioning the divine will and intent. The serpent contends that God is not worthy of trust, he engages in duplicity. The woman examines the empirical evidence (the tree was *"good for food, a delight to the eyes"*) and succumbs. Even more important is the *nature* of the temptation. Although often misconstrued that the woman desired to become *man*, the text offers no such reading. The woman's temptation is far *greater—she desires to become God!*

The question residing below the surface of Genesis 1–2 now emerges full force. Created in the image of God, will humans be content with simply *being the image*, or will they desire to *become gods* themselves? Will they be content with dominion of the earth, or will they seek complete dominion and total control? These questions go to the core of our existence as humans. Like Adam and Eve, humanity constantly strives for *something* or some *knowledge* that will make God either unnecessary or irrelevant. We long to become our own god! Genesis 3 paints in tragic colors the outcome of that quest.

Although the tree of knowledge of good and evil has been variously understood, two interpretations seem most compelling within the immediate context. Grammatically, the Hebrew construction ("good and evil") may be an example of merismus. (Merismus is a construction where the totality is stated by expressing the extremities [see 2 Samuel 14:17]. For example, one might say, "I've been everywhere" by saying "north, south, east, west.") Thus, good and evil equal "everything," total knowledge. The temptation is trenchant. If we possessed all knowledge, would God become unnecessary? Is that the difference between God and us—total vs. partial knowledge? A second interpretation may be even more compelling. "Good and evil" may specifically intend "good (for me)" and "evil (for me)." That is, eating of the tree enables the eaters to determine for themselves what is harmful or beneficial. Again, the implications are powerful. To this point, we have been presented an all-powerful Creator who has not only created us, but has also chosen to enter into a personal relationship with us. As Creator, he knows us better than we know ourselves, and knows what is best for us. The serpent claims that partaking of this fruit will make God obsolete. Humans will now have the capacity to determine for themselves what is in their best interests. They can make their own way in the world.

The scene closes as it began, with a reference to human nakedness. However, the larger context enveloping that nakedness has dramatically changed. Where human nakedness carried no shame in 2:25, shame will soon dominate the landscape. Ironically, the man and woman do have their "eyes opened"; however, what they discover is their *vulnerability*. They desperately attempt to resolve their dilemma through the tailoring of clothing.

The Garden Lost (3:8-24)

Absent from the preceding scene, God now reappears. This couple with *opened eyes* now *hears* God walking in the late afternoon. Afraid, they hide. God calls Adam and begins to question him. The questions are rhetorical; the Creator of the universe is neither uninformed nor misinformed.

> *But the LORD God called to the man, and said to him,*
> *"Where are you?" He said, "I heard the sound of you in the gar-*
> *den, and I was afraid, because I was naked; and I hid myself." He*
> *said, "Who told you that you were naked?" Have you eaten from*
> *the tree of which I commanded you not to eat?" The man said,*
> *"The woman **whom you gave to be with me**, she gave me fruit*
> *from the tree, and I ate." Then the LORD God said to the woman,*
> *"What is this that you have done?" The woman said, "The ser-*
> *pent tricked me, and I ate"* (3:9-13, emphasis added).

The dialogue is intriguing. Adam, silent in the previous scene, now becomes verbose; however, he fails to directly answer the divine questions! His language is telling, causing us to wonder whether Adam is suggesting God himself is to blame for this event! The woman, having spoken at length in the preceding scene, answers the divine question succinctly and acknowledges that she has been tricked. The oneness of the man and the woman at the conclusion of Genesis 2 has suffered a serious rupture.

Punishment follows swiftly and in reverse order to the questioning. Each recipient (serpent, woman, man) receives a two-part punishment. The snake is deemed guilty without a trial. The craftiest of animals becomes the most cursed of animals. The serpent will crawl upon its belly and eat dust; it will experience a fundamentally hostile relationship with the human realm. In that relationship of animosity, the serpent will fare poorly.

Unlike the serpent, neither the woman nor the man is cursed. The woman receives punishment for having listened to a creature rather than the Creator.

> *"I will **greatly increase** your pangs in childbearing;*
> *in pain you shall bring forth children,*
> ***yet your desire shall be for your husband,***
> ***and he shall rule over you"***
> (3:16, emphasis added).

Contrary to popular opinion, her punishment is not childbearing; rather, it is that giving birth will only occur through excruciating pain. In her quest to become her own god and determine for herself what is beneficial and harmful, the woman now will experience the painful struggle to create life apart from the Creator of life. Her second punishment has generated significant discussion, with numerous interpretations offered. A fundamental issue involves whether we read this second statement as a *prescriptive* or *descriptive* declaration. If the line is *prescriptive* (i.e., prescribing the way life should be), then Genesis 3 trumps Genesis 2. Whereas in Genesis 2 God declared that the man—woman relationship should be one of equality, he now declares that it will be one of inequality—woman will be "ruled" by man. If the line is *descriptive* (i.e., simply describing the way life typically will be), then this line simply acknowledges a fundamental tension and struggle in the man—woman relationship. Put otherwise, female subordination is due not to God's intended order in creation, but to *human sin* and the *desire* to be one's own god! It is important that we notice the text states the woman's desire will be for her husband, not her *subjection*. Further, we have earlier seen in Genesis 1 that "rule" involves taking responsibility for another. Just as God rules the universe and entrusts his earth to the rule of his human creatures, so here we might assume God intends that the man take responsibility for the woman (something he has yet to do in Genesis 3).

Reading this passage against its ancient backdrop may shed further light. In our modern western world, childbirth and delivery, while painful, have become relatively risk free. We live in a world of Cesarean sections and pre- and post-natal intensive care units. However, in the ancient world, the single most dangerous event in which a woman could participate was childbirth! This text may simply acknowledge that women will continue to desire their husbands, putting their lives at significant risk through pregnancy and childbirth, and that men will continue to take responsibility for them. (For further discussion, see below.)

The man receives the lengthiest address. Having listened to his wife rather than God, he receives a dual punishment. Interestingly, though he is not cursed, the earth is cursed because of him!

> "Because you have listened to the voice of your wife,
>   and have eaten of the tree
>   about which I commanded you,
> 'You shall not eat of it,'
>   cursed is the ground because of you;

in toil you shall eat of it all the days of your life;
thorns and thistles it shall bring forth for you;
and you shall eat the plants of the field.
By the sweat of your face
you shall eat bread
until you return to the ground,
for out of it you were taken;
you are dust,
and to dust you shall return" (3:17-19).

The contrast with Genesis 2 is striking. Whereas in Genesis 2 the man was given meaningful and manageable work, he now faces the impossible task of tending the whole earth! Worse yet, the cursed earth will only give up its produce after much struggle. The simplicity of plucking fruit and eating is replaced by the time consuming and tedious activity of turning grain into bread. As often as not, the earth will produce inedible weeds. Meaningful vocation that brings satisfaction has been supplanted by the drudgery of toilsome work. Further, the man will experience a constant awareness of mortality. Though likely previously mortal, rebellion against the Creator of life forces death to the center of that ruptured relationship. We cannot help but wonder whether this human combination of clay from the earth and breath from God now experiences more keenly the frailty of the earth than the empowering presence of God.

The final scene demonstrates both the seriousness and loving graciousness of God. Having failed miserably to heed God's word regarding the disastrous consequences of eating the tree of knowledge of good and evil, God realizes the tree of life may create even greater problems for this frail couple. He now eliminates the possibility of another tragic mistake by physically distancing them from the garden. However, his punishment is not without compassion. God replaces their inadequate clothing (leaves) with functional clothing (animal skins). Life has changed—the animals entrusted to the man must now provide clothing for humankind.

In contrast to the larger ancient Near East, where conflict is a *built-in* assumption of the universe, in Genesis 2-3 conflict is the result of human rebellion. Human questioning of divine intent and motive propels the world into disorder, alienation, and struggle.

Disharmony supplants harmony; disunity replaces unity. The declared blessings pronounced by God withdraw in the face of curse; the intended fertility is thrown into ambiguity (with the rupture in the male—female relationship). The position of humans in the created order is now fraught with uncertainty and anxiety. With the expulsion from the garden, the narrative is thrown into suspense.

Excursus: Male and Female

Because of the various uses made of this narrative in contemporary gender discussions, some specific comments seem in order. Not surprisingly, the discussion usually begins with the interpretation of the woman's "desire" for her husband. A popular interpretation argues that the woman's desire, whatever it may be, will be subjected to that of her husband. Making that interpretation more specific, some contend that the woman's desire specifically entails her drive to dominate her husband and the relationship. Conversely, others contend that the woman's desire involves primarily her (sexual) desire for intimacy with her husband. The first two interpretations assume a hierarchical reading of Genesis 2.

Although numerous arguments have been marshaled in support of male superiority and female subordination, the following list provides a sampling of those arguments most frequently cited.

- A *male* God creates first man and last woman; first means superior and last means inferior (subordinate).
- Woman is created for the sake of man—a helpmate to cure his loneliness.
- Contrary to nature, woman comes out of man—she is denied even her natural function of birthing (that function being given to man).
- Taken out of man, woman has a derivative, rather than autonomous, existence.
- Woman is the rib of man, dependent upon him for life.
- Man names woman and thus has power over her.
- Man leaves his father's family in order to set up through his wife another patriarchal unit.
- Woman tempted man to disobey and thus she is responsible for sin in the world; she is untrustworthy, gullible, and simpleminded.

- Woman is cursed by pain in childbirth; pain in childbirth is a more severe punishment than man's struggle with the soil, signifying that woman's sin is greater than man's.
- Woman's desire for man is God's way of keeping her faithful and submissive to her husband.
- God gives man the right to rule over the woman.

In response, several problems arise from a hierarchical reading of Genesis 2:

- From a literary standpoint, Genesis 2 exhibits *ring composition;* i.e., the order intends not a move from superiority to inferiority, but from incompleteness to completeness. The two most crucial components of the narrative are at the beginning (man) and end (woman). Woman is the climax and culmination of the narrative—she is the crowning work of creation!
- Eve's derivation from Adam does not presume subordination, or else Adam, derived from earth, would find himself inferior to it.
- Creation from the rib implies equality; woman is intended to stand side by side with man.
- Reading the language of helpmate as implying subordination defies the lexical evidence for the term.
- The grammatical evidence for Adam's naming of Eve reflects more the world of recognition and discovery than the world of dominion and subordination. In naming the woman, Adam is not determining her identity, but rejoicing in what God has done.
- The language of 2:24 ("leave . . . cleave") reverberates with covenantal significance. In Genesis 2, woman was created for meaningful and fulfilling companionship, companionship best reflected in a covenantal relationship of both partners giving fully of themselves to the other. Eve and Adam have shattered that wonderful covenant relationship through their desire to be their own gods.
- There is no indication the woman's succumbing to temptation was in any way related to separation from her husband, nor to usurping his authority. Rather, it involves exalting herself above the Creator to determine for herself right and wrong.

■ One expects the statement about desire to have some connection with childbirth pain. In the ancient world, the ability to alleviate the pain of childbirth and the potentially fatal consequences of labor and delivery was absent. The possibility for the loss of the mother's life during pregnancy and (especially) delivery were staggering.

Without question, Genesis 3:16 has significant hermeneutical implications for contemporary believers. Again, numerous hermeneutical implications have been suggested:

■ The subordination of woman is a *creation ordinance* (i.e., God's ideal from the beginning), but through sin this original form of hierarchy was *distorted and corrupted* and must be restored by the gospel.
■ Subordination is a *creation ordinance*; however, 3:16 reflects *not a distortion* of subordination but a reaffirmation of subordination as a blessing and comfort to woman in her difficulties as mother.
■ The subordination of 3:16 is a blessing rather than a curse; however, subordination is not a creation ordinance.
■ Subordination did not exist prior to sin; further, the statement of subordination of 3:16 intends only a description of God's will for subsequent husband-wife relationships.
■ Subordination did not exist prior to the sin; however 3:16 is *prescriptive*, not merely *descriptive*.

Genesis 2–3 demands that we reflect long and hard about our relationship to God and to each other. Yahweh's intent for creation is ruptured. Through challenging the divine design for creation, the human couple tragically alters each of their relationships: 1) their relationship with their Creator; 2) their relationship with each other; 3) their relationship with the rest of the created order. Where once harmony, productivity, and meaning reigned, now pain, struggle, and potential meaningless life dominate. The contrast could not be more poignantly drawn. In their desire to circumvent their need for a Sovereign Lord, they achieve not fulfillment but become keenly aware of the weakness and vulnerability of their creatureliness. They are creatures; even knowledge cannot remove that. In their relationship to each other, equality and mutual concern and care is replaced by struggle, conflict, and obsession with hierarchical order. Finally, the rest of creation, given to them for enjoyment and sustenance, now deals them endless toil and backbreaking labor. The joy and freedom of life under the protective wing of the Creator has given way to a constant awareness of struggle and the omnipresence of mortality and finitude. However, the story continues, for the God of Genesis 1–3 is a God of infinite grace and mercy, a God who repeatedly calls his creation to realign with his purposes and intent. Most dramatically, he ultimately exhibits that posture himself in the gift of his own Son.

Finding Ourselves in Genesis 2–3

Genesis 2–3 provides us with a powerful account of the nature of God, the relationship of God to his human creatures, and the relation of human creatures to one another. Whereas God is presented primarily through the metaphor of a sovereign monarch in Genesis 1, in Genesis 2–3 several images arise. As God creates, he is a potter sculpting the dust of the earth into a man. As gardener, he plants a luxurious garden to address the physical needs of this creature. As surgeon and architect, he crafts a woman from man. With the completion of creation in Genesis 2, humans have vocation (caring for the garden), permission (eating of the garden) and prohibition (refraining from that which will harm them). Perhaps most significantly, they have community (2:23-25). Humankind has not been created to live in isolation, but in a community of harmony and mutuality.

Genesis 2–3 calls us to re-examine our understanding of our relationship with God, with each other, and with the world in which we live. Like Adam and Eve, God questions us. God's questioning has little to do with seeking unknown information; it rather involves self-revelation. As we answer God's questions, "Where are you?" "What have you done?" (and later, "Why are you angry?" [4:6]), we see ourselves as God sees us. Like the first man and woman, we come to realize that our language of fidelity and acceptance often gives way to analysis and calculation. God becomes less a conversational partner and more an object of discussion. The language of trust and obedience gives way to questioning and suspicion of God's intentions and motives. We begin to listen to another, rather than to God.

Genesis 2–3 reminds us that such movement is typically neither single nor immediate. Rather, we gradually move from one stage to another. Just as Eve deliberated over the fruit and analyzed its benefits (with no mention of its potential harm), so we often rationalize our move away from trust in God to exaltation of ourselves. Genesis 2–3 powerfully reminds us that sin (though unmentioned in Genesis 3!) is first and foremost a heart problem. Just as the external act of eating the fruit is simply the final stage in a progressive series of steps away from trust in God, so Jesus reminds us in the Sermon on the Mount that sin begins in the heart, only later manifesting itself in external misbehavior.

■ Why is sin not mentioned in Genesis 3? Or, is it?
■ How is sin a "heart" problem?

Genesis 3 addresses a core issue of our lives.

■ Can we trust this God who has created us and claims to have our best interests at heart?
■ Can we trust that what we may perceive as benefits may ultimately be detriments to a full and meaningful life?

Genesis 3 reminds us that the *essence of temptation is the desire to become like God*, to live not under the command to be responsible, but to decide for ourselves what responsibility is. Often, knowledge is the intoxicating elixir in that potion, for knowledge entices us to think that we can determine for ourselves what is beneficial or detrimental for us. Against the backdrop of such questions, we may read Genesis 3 differently. Just as we inappropriately obsess in chapter two over the prohibition God declares rather than celebrating the permission he bestows, so in chapter three we often question the punishments, rather than marveling that God allows this rebellious couple to live! When the facts warrant death, God decrees life.

Genesis 2–3 reminds us of the pervasive impact of sin upon our lives. When we decide to become our own god, every aspect of human life is touched—our marriages, our sexuality, our labor, our beginnings (birth) and endings (death). A devastating consequence of rebellion against God is that blame becomes a central feature of our lives. Realizing that we are ill equipped to truly manage our own lives, we find ourselves constantly seeking scape-goats to blame and thus deflect responsibility. Adam's first move is telling—he blames Eve (and implicitly God!) for his actions. Ironically, some students of Scripture read Genesis 3 in this manner. Some will read the text and "blame" Eve; others will "blame" Adam. The Apostle Paul's words seem appropriate at this point. Whereas in 1 Timothy 2 Paul focuses upon Eve, and in Romans 5 he focuses upon Adam, in Romans 3 he focuses upon us:

> But now, apart from law, the righteousness of God has been disclosed, and is attested by the law and the prophets, the righteousness of God through faith in Jesus Christ for all who believe. For there is no distinction, **since all have sinned and fall short of the glory of God**; they are now justified by his grace as a gift, through the redemption that is in Christ Jesus, whom God put forward as a sacrifice of atonement by his blood, effective through faith. He did this to show his righteousness, because in his divine forbearance he had passed over the sins previously committed; it was to prove at the present time that he himself is righteous and that he justifies the one who has faith in Jesus (Romans 3:21-26, emphasis added).

Genesis 2–3 deals with perennial issues of life and death. Where a strong Christian tradition views our present world as the tragic consequences of a woman who was tempted and fell short, a significant Jewish rabbinic tradition views this present world as the consequences of human freedom! In a similar vein, Genesis 2–3 may provide us with a theological critique of "anxiety." As humans, God has created us with the freedom to choose for or against him. Ironically, such freedom generates questioning, questioning whether this all-powerful Creator is *for* us or *against* us! Such questioning results in anxiety. In Genesis 3, we see Adam and Eve attempt to solve that anxiety and put themselves in a place where their lives will no longer be totally dependent upon God's promises. Genesis 3 portrays the tragic consequences of attempting to solve human anxiety by circumventing God's providence.

■ Like Adam and Eve, we often are tempted to solve our anxieties through means other than trust and dependence upon God. Give some examples of this in your life.

We live surrounded by a culture that feebly attempts to solve anxiety through psychological, economic, or cosmetic means. Against such a backdrop, the words of Jesus seem most appropriate:

> *"Therefore I tell you, do not worry about your life, what you will eat or what you will drink, or about your body, what you will wear. Is not life more than food, and the body more than clothing? Look at the birds of the air; they neither sow nor reap nor gather into barns, and yet your heavenly Father feeds them. Are you not of more value than they? And can any of you by worrying add a single hour to your span of life? And why do you worry about clothing? Consider the lilies of the field, how they grow; they neither toil nor spin, yet I tell you, even Solomon in all his glory was not clothed like one of these. But if God so clothes the grass of the field, which is alive today and tomorrow is thrown into the oven, will he not much more clothe you—you of little faith? Therefore do not worry, saying, 'What will we eat?' or 'What will we drink?' or 'What will we wear?' For it is the Gentiles who strive for all these things; and indeed your heavenly Father knows that you need all these things. But strive first for the kingdom of God and his righteousness, and all these things will be given to you as well.*
>
> *"So do not worry about tomorrow, for tomorrow will bring worries of its own. Today's trouble is enough for today* (Matthew 6:25-34).

Genuine removal of anxiety occurs when we entrust ourselves to the Creator who promises to bless and care for us. In that setting we find and experience true life, life dominated not by anxiety, but by peace and joy and love.

CHAPTER 4

Life Outside the Garden

(Genesis 4–11)

enesis 4–11 depicts for us in graphic detail the nature of life "outside the garden." We see in the remaining chapters of the primeval history the tragic consequences of choosing to direct our own lives and decide for ourselves right and wrong. Although life is forever changed, it is not hopeless. Human hubris and desire for autonomy is more than matched by God's persistent love and relentless desire to have a relationship with all elements of his creation (most especially his human creatures).

Genesis 1–11 can be structured in a variety of ways. On the one hand, Genesis 1 presents us with a panoramic view of creation, a view counterbalanced by the detailed look of Genesis 2–3. Genesis 2–3 can be read as a (mis)matched set—Genesis 2 reflects God's design for his human subjects; Genesis 3 depicts the tragic consequences of human choices against God's design. From another vantage point, Genesis 3 introduces a series of narratives with a common theological structure. In Genesis 3–11, four narratives are presented: Adam and Eve; Cain and Abel; Noah and the Flood; the Tower of Babel. Interestingly, the narrative of the flood is both preceded and followed by a genealogy. The preceding genealogy (Genesis 5) details the lineages of two prominent ancestors—Cain and Seth. The following genealogy (Genesis 10) details the genealogical ordering of the various nations that will result from Noah's family.

The theological pattern of each of the four narratives is similar. Each narrative has a threefold theological structure—sin, punishment, and renewal. Each narrative begins with a detailing of the sin committed. In each case, the sin is essentially rebellion. A segment of God's humanity will choose self-rule rather than divine control. God will respond with an appropriate punishment. However, the final chapter of God's interaction with humanity is never punishment. In each case he will start over with his creatures. In this theological pattern, the renewal typically comes in the form of a child. The following chart depicts the theological arrangement of the narratives.

	Sin	Punishment	Renewal
Adam and Eve	Desire to become become like God > eating fruit	Painful childbirth; Grueling toil; Expulsion from garden	Birth of Cain
Cain and Abel	Anger > Murder	Wanderer	Birth of Seth
Noah and Flood	Social Violence	Flood	Noah (descendants)
Tower of Babel	Self-generated Security; Fame	Scattering; Communication confusion	Abraham

Cain and Abel (Genesis 4)

Genesis 4 details the crime and punishment of Cain (vv. 1-16) and the descendants of Cain (vv. 17-26). The story begins on an upbeat note. Adam and Eve, having only recently experienced the loss of the beautiful garden, now experience the joy of a newborn child. At her delivery, Eve acknowledges her dependency upon God when she names the child. She calls him Cain (*qayin*), saying, *"I have acquired/produced (qaniti) a man with the help of the Lord."* A second pregnancy produces a second son; this son receives an ominous name—Abel ("ephemeral, nothingness").

The two sons embark on different career paths. Cain becomes a farmer, a tiller of the soil (like his father); Abel embraces the life of a shepherd. At some unspecified point in time, and for some unspecified reason, Cain decides to offer some of his produce to God. Abel decides to do likewise.

> *In the course of time Cain brought to the LORD an offering of the fruit of the ground, and Abel for his part brought of the firstlings of his flock, their fat portions. And the LORD had regard for Abel and his offering, but for Cain and his offering he had no regard. So Cain was very angry, and his countenance fell (4:3-5).*

The succinctness of the text both fascinates and frustrates us. The text provides us no explicit rationale for the approval of the latter sacrifice and the disapproval of the former. Although numerous suggestions have been offered, the answer may lie in the simplicity of the language itself. The text states simply that Cain gave *something* of his produce; Abel, on the other hand, gave *"the firstlings, [and] their fat portions."* That is, Abel gave the best of his best! In contrast to Cain, who chose not to give the firstfruits of his produce, Abel gives the choicest. Against this backdrop, the divine response is telling. God simply *disregards* an offering that received little *regard* from its donor!

In actuality, the focus of the text lies elsewhere. Whereas we may desire to know the reason for the Lord's response, the text wants us to grapple with *Cain's response* to the Lord's reaction. Not receiving the reaction he expected from God, Cain becomes angry. Although some suggest Cain's anger is directed against his brother (and interpret the text as a reflection on sibling jealousy), I would suggest Cain's anger is first and foremost directed at God. Cain, apparently seeking approval from God, becomes angry. Either unwilling or unable to resolve his anger, he looks about for a scapegoat on whom he can vent. Abel becomes the innocent recipient of Cain's faulty relationship with God. At an opportune moment, he slays his brother Abel in the field; the tiller of the ground has now sown the blood of his brother on that ground. The action is simple and straightforward; the ensuing dialogue between God and Cain is riveting.

> The LORD said to Cain, "Why are you angry, and why has your countenance fallen? If you do well, will you not be accepted? And if you do not do well, sin is lurking at the door; its desire is for you, but you must master it." . . . Then the LORD said to Cain, "Where is your brother Abel?" He said, "I do not know; am I my brother's keeper?" And the LORD said, "What have you done? Listen; your brother's blood is crying out to me from the ground! And now you are cursed from the ground, which has opened its mouth to receive your brother's blood from your hand. When you till the ground, it will no longer yield to you its strength; you will be a fugitive and a wanderer on the earth" (4:6-7, 9-12).

Cain becomes the first person to whom *sin* is attributed. It is noteworthy that God presents sin as a choice. We either choose for or against sin. We dare not miss, however, that the choice is difficult. Sin is graphically portrayed as a predator ready to pounce (see Jeremiah 5:6). Sin has an enticing, possessive, aggressive character that must be resisted. Tragically, Cain chooses poorly and thus himself becomes a predator stalking Abel.

Like Adam and Eve, God's response follows swiftly and decisively. The punishment fits the crime. This tiller of the soil who has shed blood upon the cursed earth now receives a divine curse. That which is most precious to him is taken—he will wander throughout the earth denied the very land he longs to farm. The finale is striking. This wanderer (*nad*) wanders eastward until he establishes a city in the land of "Wandering" (*nod*). Though bereft of land and thinking the Lord has abandoned him, he receives a final word of comfort. God reaches out to Cain with compassion and "marks" him for protection. Though Cain may regard himself separated from the presence of the Lord, the alienation apparently is not total.

The intimate relationship between Genesis 3 and 4 is striking. Where Genesis 3 addresses the havoc that rebellion against God wreaks on marital relationships, Genesis 4 recounts the devastating impact sin has upon fraternal relationships. Adam and Eve grapple with the "heady" reality of being created at the "top of the heap" of creation, yet less than the Creator. They choose to remove that gap and become God. Cain inherits the same lofty position. However, he attempts to remove any competition to that relationship. The irony is poignant. It is our *exalted status*, this gift of grace from God, that has within it the potential to destroy our relationship with God and with each other. Adam and Eve experience "expulsion" (*garash*) from the garden; Cain experiences "expulsion" (*garash*) from the soil. The earth is the recipient of a divine curse because of the first couple's rebellion; Cain receives a curse for the blood shed upon the cursed earth. Just as Eve will *desire* an intimate relationship with her husband, so God warns Cain that sin *desires* control of his life, but he must resist. God uses the power of rhetorical questions to get Adam, Eve, and Cain to confront the reality of their wrong choices ("Where are you?" "What have you done?" "Where is your brother?"). Where Adam and Eve desired to *become like God*, Cain *plays God*. The level of rebellion is rising— where Adam excused his sin; Cain denies his. Adam hid, fearful of God's presence; Cain initially refuses his culpability and rejects any responsibility for his brother.

The aftermath of this scene haunts us. We meet Cain's descendants, one in particular. With the descendants of Cain we encounter the beginnings of *civilization*. Cain's descendants build cities, invent music, and manufacture tools. From Cain's descendants also comes the first case of bigamy. The initial absence of remorse from Cain festers into bombastic defiance in his descendant Lamech. Lamech, husband of two wives, completely misapplies the divine response to Cain. He boasts that if Cain receives a sevenfold protection from God after having committed cold-blooded murder, surely he will receive a seventy-sevenfold protection for justifiable homicide! The tear in the social fabric has dramatically widened. Lamech ignores the vision of monogamy (2:24) and boasts of the level of retribution he has inflicted following a mere wound. We cannot help but wonder whether the technological advancements Cain's descendants have produced do not carry an accompanying increase in *uncivilized* social behavior.

As with the conclusion of the Adam and Eve narrative, the conclusion of the Cain and Abel narrative offers renewal. The final word introduces us to a third child born to Eve—Seth. Like the birth of Cain, she acknowledges the activity of God in the birth. She names him *"Seth (sheth), for she said, 'God has appointed (shath) for me another child instead of Abel.'"*

From this son, hope springs. In contrast to the firstborn Cain who introduces the technological marvels of civilization with their dangerous downside, Seth and his descendants worship the Lord: *"To Seth also a son was born, and he named him Enosh. At that time people began to invoke the name of the LORD."* Genesis 5 provides a quick overview of the Sethites. They are characterized by long lives (although no one lives to see quadruple digits). If Lamech epitomizes the presumptuous folly and excess of the Cainite lineage, Enoch (and in anticipatory fashion, Noah) epitomizes the faithful obedience of the Sethite lineage. Enoch walks with God, and so avoids the shadow of mortality that hangs over the rest of humanity. The genealogy concludes with the introduction of the key character in the ensuing narrative—Noah.

Noah and the Flood (Genesis 6–9)

Although a most popular reading of Genesis 1–11 highlights Genesis 3, labeling it *"the Fall,"* a straightforward reading of these eleven chapters suggest we take seriously the account of the flood. The importance and centrality of the flood to these early chapters is evidenced by at least three features. More space is devoted to the narrating of the flood and its consequences than any other event in the primeval history. Second, the flood narrative is structurally "wrapped" by genealogies. One genealogy immediately precedes the flood narrative; another immediately follows it. Third, unlike the other narratives in Genesis 3–11 that give one paragraph to the initial rebellion triggering the divine response of punishment, the flood narrative begins with two introductions.

We dare not miss the incredible change in conditions at the outset of this narrative. The punishment we encounter is cataclysmic, catastrophic, and all encompassing. Accordingly, the narrative opens with a depiction of human sin that is all encompassing. Simply put, humanity is out of control. The first scene (Genesis 6:1-4) is extremely enigmatic and stirs the imagination. We read that the sons of God intermarry with the daughters of man, resulting in heroic warriors. Understanding this enigmatic text depends on our identification of each of these groups. Although some suggest that the sin depicted here is the intermarriage of the materialistic and worldly descendants of Cain ("daughters of men") with the godly descendants of Seth ("sons of God"), this language is nowhere else attested in Scripture with such a nuance. Consistently throughout Scripture, "sons of God" is a term for divine beings (see Job 1:6; 2:1; Psalms 29:1; 89:6 [7]; Daniel 3:25; cf. Psalm 82:1). This would suggest the issue in this opening scene involves the intermarriage between divine beings and human beings. The question mark in this interpretation involves why the narrative makes no mention of the punishment of the divine beings. To this question we will return.

The second narrative is clear and straightforward:

> The LORD saw that the **wickedness** of humankind was **great** in the earth, and that **every inclination** of the **thoughts** of their **hearts** was **only evil continually** (6:5, emphasis added).

Two observations merit comment. First, we cannot help but recognize that we are no longer talking of the single sins of a single individual (or couple). Rather, the text stresses that the entire earth is filled with rampant rebellion and evil. Second, the terminology is telling. The language employed is language used elsewhere in the Bible to depict social violence. That is, the evil that fills the earth consists of social injustice and violent treatment of one another (see

6:11-13). This observation is not insignificant. In actuality, the flood is a violent response to a violent society bent on self-destruction.

The flood is God's response to such abusive behavior. While our attention might drift toward the extent of the divine response, the text first forces us to consider the motivation of the divine response.

> And the LORD was **sorry** that he had made humankind on the earth, and it **grieved him to his heart**. So the LORD said, "I will blot out from the earth the human beings I have created—people together with animals and creeping things and birds of the air, for **I am sorry** that I have made them" (6:6-7, emphasis added).

The punishing flood is rooted not in divine anger, but in *grief!* In a very real sense, *the Fall* is complete. That segment of creation in which God expressed such delight and pride becomes the only element of creation he ever regrets creating! Humans, his pride and joy, have become his sorrow and regret. The expanse of the flood pales in comparison to the expanse of the gulf between the divine intent for creation and the human response to that intent. The evil heart of humanity troubles the heart of God. Violence engulfs God's noblest creature. In response, God determines to begin again.

The arrangement of the flood narrative is noteworthy. Like Genesis 2–3, the composition of the text manifests ring composition. That is, the second half of the narrative is presented in reverse fashion to the first half. In the first half of the narrative the waters rise; in the second half they recede. The "hinge" in the narrative is God's remembrance of Noah. The outline (Outline 2) on page 68 makes this clear.

The format of the narrative is similar to Genesis 1. Repeatedly we encounter a divine command followed by the execution of that command. As we read, we cannot help but realize that we have *returned* to Genesis 1. In a very real sense, God is *reversing* his creation. Just as Genesis 1 began with God pushing dry land up out of a watery mass, so in Genesis 6–9 God submerges that dry land. Having completely submerged the earth, he then raises it from the watery chaos and starts again. The flood narrative is *creation revisited*. God is re-creating his earth.

Numerous parallels appear between the narrative of creation and the flood. Creation begins with the *wind* (spirit) of God moving

---

OUTLINE 2 ■

(A) God's creation is riddled with violence (6:11-12)
  (B) God's opening declaration—the resolution to destroy (6:13-22)
    (C) God's second address—the command to enter ark (7:1-10)
      (D) The flood begins (7:11-16)
        (E) The floodwaters rise (7:17-24)
          (F) GOD REMEMBERS NOAH
        (E) The floodwaters recede (8:1-5)
      (D) The earth dries (8:6-14)
    (C) God's third address—the command to leave the ark (8:15-19)
  (B) God's resolves to preserve order (8:20-22)
(A) God's final declaration—a call for blessing and peace (9:1-17)

---

across the face of the waters; God remembers Noah and causes a wind to blow across the waters so that they subside (8:1). Both narratives conclude with a call to humankind to *"be fruitful and multiply"* (1:28; 8:17). Human sin results in a *cursed earth* (3:17-19; 4:11-12; 5:29); after the flood God promises never to curse the earth again (8:21-22). The earth will be affected more by divine faithfulness than by human sin. In both scenes humankind receives a blessing from God (1:28-30; 9:1). Both scenes entrust the animal realm to the care and protection of humankind (1:28-30; 2:18-20; 9:2-5). Perhaps most importantly, humanity *after the flood* is still created in the image of God (1:26; 9:6).

With the exit of Noah from the ark, we enter a new world with a new beginning. Punishment is never the final word from God. God is faithful to his promises—he *remembers Noah*. He marks his faithfulness to his promises through the placement of his (rain)bow in the sky. Read against the larger backdrop of the ancient world, the rainbow is nothing less than a symbol of the military bow of the Lord. God has "waged war" against his creation. He now hangs up his bow in the sky to remind all humankind that he will never wage war against it again. Just as creation concludes with God *resting* over his creation as Sovereign Lord, so the flood concludes with God *resting* his bow.

Creation begins again with *righteous* Noah and his family. In a world given to violence and destructive behavior, Noah lives in right relationship with God. The rightness of his relationship manifests itself in his obedience to the divine call. Noah responds faithfully to the faithful Creator. However, righteousness does not imply perfection. No sooner do we read of Noah's sacrifice of praise than we find Noah experiencing the debilitating effects of fermented grapes. Noah, drunk from wine, lies naked in his tent. His condition makes him oblivious to the *shame* Adam and Eve experienced when they realized the full implications of their nakedness. In a poignant moment, his son Ham rejects the option of manifesting filial respect for his father and chooses instead to make light of his father's condition. In contrast, Noah's sons Shem and Japheth treat their father with respect and loving care. Just as Cain's descendants manifested tragically the behavioral characteristics of their ancestor, so Ham's descendants will reap the consequences of their ancestor's disrespect.

Tower of Babel (Genesis 11)

The earth is once again fully peopled. The question arises, will this new humanity, created in the image of God, learn from its ancestors? We find the answer to this question in Genesis 11. Moving about in the east, humankind determines to settle. They locate in the plain of Shinar (ancient Babylon) and decide to construct for themselves a city. Our minds quickly race back to our first introduction to city builders—the descendants of Cain. These new wanderers desire to build a city, and station a tower in its midst, a tower "with its top in the heavens." (Ironically, God will eventually have to *come down* to observe this tower!) The rationale for these building plans is striking.

"Come, let us build ourselves a city, and a tower with its top in the heavens, and let us make a name for ourselves; otherwise we shall be scattered abroad upon the face of the whole earth" (11:4).

The motivation of the builders seems twofold—hubris ("make a name for ourselves") and fear ("lest we be scattered"). In Hebrew the expression "to make a name" denotes "to become famous." Much Jewish interpretation interprets the motivation of the Babel builders simply as an unwillingness to fulfill God's injunction to "multiply, fill the earth, and subdue" it. In contrast, much Christian interpretation considers the Babel narrative to reflect that Promethean impulse to storm the heavens and supplant God.

Perhaps the truth lies somewhere between. In Genesis 3, Adam and Eve were tempted with what may be the most fundamental temptation to all humanity—the desire to become like God. In Genesis 11, we see that temptation played out on a corporate level. The Babel builders seek to achieve their own security. For them, security seemingly has to do with place. By localizing themselves in one place as one people, they can avoid the dangers of migration and its attendant insecurities. For them, a city provides the solution. The tower, reaching to the heavens, addresses a second human ambition—the ambition to escape the limitations of the human condition. They desire fame and recognition for their own accomplishments. (Again, we are somewhat close to the themes found in the Cainite genealogy—the descendants of Cain are noted for their *own* accomplishments, not for their relationship with God.)

The reaction of God is appropriate to the crime. In response to their desire for security, God denies them the security rooted in one place and one people. They are scattered and made multi-lingual. In response to their desire for fame, they go down in history *nameless* (how many people from the Tower of Babel episode can you name?).

Earlier we mentioned that the flood narrative is encircled by genealogies. In like manner, the episode of the Tower of Babel is surrounded by genealogies. Immediately preceding the narrative of the tower is a genealogy commonly entitled the "Table of Nations" (Genesis 10). Painted against a large backdrop, it outlines the nations that result from the descendants of Noah and his sons. Situated immediately before the Tower of Babel, it anticipates the narrative that will detail how these nations came to be scattered across the face of the earth.

Like the preceding narratives, the final chapter in the Babel story is not punishment. Rather, it is renewal. Once again, God returns to start over with these fickle creatures seemingly bent on self-destruction. Renewal appears first in the genealogy immediately following the Tower of Babel. In that genealogy, we are introduced to a new figure—Abraham. As we will later discover, Abraham will receive the promise of a *great name*, something the Babel builders desperately sought for themselves but failed to achieve.

Excursus—Genesis 4–11 & the Ancient Near East

The ancient Near East has produced a treasure trove of documents for contemporary students of the Bible. These documents elucidate the larger context in which God's people lived. They provide invaluable information about how differently Israel's neighbors understood the divine realm and the relationship of humans to that divine realm. Three artifacts deserve special mention against the backdrop of Genesis 3–11. The first two are texts, the third a monument.

The story of *Atrahasis* is a well-known document from the ancient Near East. Although often called the "Babylonian story of the flood," it is perhaps more appropriately labeled the "Babylonian Genesis." Though addressing similar themes, the theological vision is dramatically different. When we compare *Atrahasis* with the opening chapters of the Bible, we can see how differently ancient Israel understood God and his relationship to his people from the Babylonians.

The story line of *Atrahasis*, though at points a bit unclear, is relatively straightforward. The story begins with the creation of humankind and the world. Like *Enuma Elish*, humans were created to "solve a problem" in the divine realm. The "high gods" (*Annunaki*) were forcing the lesser gods (*Igigi*) to work constantly, thus denying them any chance of "rest" (a primary privilege of gods). The lesser gods revolted, set fire to their tools, and refused to continue slaving in such a *human* manner. To solve this labor strike, the high gods created humans. Henceforth, humans would be entrusted with the backbreaking work of provisioning the gods. While solving one problem, another was created. As humankind multiplied in the earth, they began to make such noise ("din") that the great gods were deprived of their sleep. Angry, Enlil (the great god) determined to diminish humankind through a devastating flood. The lesser gods, realizing their fragile status, enlisted the aid of Enki, the god of wisdom. Enki thwarted Enlil's destructive plan by forewarning a human, Atrahasis. Enki gave Atrahasis explicit instructions to enable him to save himself, his family, and representative animals. After the flood, Atrahasis offered a sacrifice to the gods in appreciation for his deliverance. Every god but Enlil recognized the need of humankind—their sole purpose was to serve the gods. To pacify Enlil, additional regulations and rules were imposed upon humankind so that they could be easily controlled.

The Epic of Gilgamesh also provides a fascinating look into the ancient world of Mesopotamia. In actuality, this epic is primarily about the exploits of Gilgamesh and addresses the issue of human mortality. Embedded within this epic tale is a short section (Tablet XI) detailing a flood. At the outset of the story, we meet Gilgamesh, an incredibly powerful king out of control. His irresponsible treatment of his subjects leads them to cry to the gods for help. The divine realm, sympathetic to the pleas of these human sufferers, makes several attempts to bring Gilgamesh under control, with little success.

However, one day the traveling companion (*Enkidu*) of Gilgamesh dies. Gilgamesh comes face to face with the inevitability of his own death. He pleads with the divine realm for life. He discovers that only one human has ever received a reprieve from mortality—Utnapishtim. Gilgamesh embarks upon a difficult and dangerous journey to discover the secret to Utnapishtim's "success." When they meet, Utnapishtim tells Gilgamesh of his survival through a devastating flood sent by the gods. The story line is similar to that just recounted from *Atrahasis* (and with some modification *Enuma Elish*). The great gods determine to destroy humanity because of the noise they are making; such a plan the lesser gods recognize as disastrous for them. The edict from the great gods is that no one may forewarn the human realm. However, Enki creatively circumvents the decree. Upon arriving on earth, Enki instructs the human Utnapishtim to enter his reed hut. Enki, the god of wisdom, next instructs the reed hut in great detail about the building of a boat and the gathering of animals and professional craftsmen. Utnapishtim "overhears" the conversation and follows Enki's instructions exactly. He and his passengers survive the onslaught of the flood. Upon their departure from the boat, they offer a sacrifice to the gods. The gods, having been deprived of food (sacrifices) for seven days, swarm the sacrifice. Though Enlil is furious, Enki is innocent—the reed hut divulged the plan!

A final piece of "help" we receive from the ancient Near East comes in the form of a monument. Ancient Mesopotamians lived in a "three-tiered universe." They envisioned their world with three levels—an underworld, a flat disc (on which we live), and an overarching dome (sky) separating the divine realm from the human realm. Since the divine realm inhabited the upper tier, proximity to the divine realm was in direct proportion to distance from the face of the flat disc. Simply put, one was closer to the gods on a mountain than in a valley. Since Mesopotamia lacked significant mountains, her inhabitants compensated by constructing *ziggurats* (towers). These pyramidal monuments with multiple staircases functioned centrally in Mesopotamian worship. Typically an altar adorned the peak of the monument. At the summit, the divine realm was within reach. As the sacrifices were offered, the gods and goddesses descended to partake of the food offered.

Read against this backdrop, the Tower of Babel takes on added meaning. Whereas a Mesopotamian would consider this tower a focal point for worship and communion with the gods, we realize that this tower is in actuality a monument to human hubris and insecurity. The Tower of "Babel" carries multiple nuances. On the one hand, this tower was rightly named. It memorialized the "confusion" (*balal*) of the languages and the people involved. However, there is likely more. The ancient capital of southern Mesopotamia, Babylon (*bab-ili/bab-ilani*) meant "gate(way) of the gods." These ziggurats, central symbols for worship, were monuments to human folly and misunderstanding.

Both *Atrahasis* and *The Epic of Gilgamesh* provide valuable insights for students of the Bible. The material is valuable, for this is the world from which Abraham and the patriarchs came. The question of *borrowing* (that is, who borrowed from whom) misses the point. These epics were known and recounted throughout the Mesopotamian river valley. The Mesopotamians apparently told and retold these stories (in several variations) with delight. Of much more importance is the theological worldview depicted in these texts. In the Mesopotamian materials we encounter a divine realm that is populated by a plethora of gods and goddesses. These deities frequently disagree and vie among themselves for power and position. They often operate out of *self-interest*. Their stance toward the human realm is mixed. At times they can manifest care and concern; not infrequently, they demonstrate capriciousness and less than honorable motives in their dealings with humanity. On the one hand, they have created these humans to serve them and meet their needs. Because of this, they often recognize the mutual need they and the human realm have for each other. On the other hand, the multiplication of human beings on the earth increases the decibel level and potential for trouble. (The terminology for the noise that these humans create may likely be a euphemism for rebellion.) The divine realm splits on the severity of this problem and how best to address it. The great gods tend to propose severe and decisive solutions (e.g., total destruction).

In Genesis 1–11, God is never dependent upon humankind for his needs. (This theme resounds clearly throughout the Old Testament, see Psalm 50.) He creates not to solve a *problem*, but solely to complete his creation in glorious fashion. Humankind is not primarily the lackey of the divine realm; it bears the very image of God. In striking contrast to the Mesopotamian vision of the deities, the God of Scripture never acts capriciously. Sole God of the universe, he is never divided in his stance toward humanity. He responds not out of anger or whim, but out of grief. He counters his human creatures, who seem prone repeatedly to make wrong choices and engage in actions that deny his place as Creator, with acts of measured discipline and renewal. In extreme cases (such as the social conditions preceding the flood) he responds severely. Yet even in these cases, divine sorrow engulfs the scene.

Finding Ourselves in Genesis 4–11

Many of us first heard the stories of Cain and Abel, Noah and the Flood, and the Tower of Babel in Sunday school. Although they continue to captivate the imagination of young children, they are not first and foremost designed for the consumption of children. These are adult stories with adult messages. The story of Cain and Abel speaks powerfully to such diverse issues as sibling rivalry, the nature and purpose of worship, and the importance of the choices we make. The story of Noah and the flood calls us to reflect deeply once again on the nature of the God we worship, the nature of righteousness, and the far-reaching consequences of our sin(fullness). The Tower of Babel calls into question our incessant longing for fame and our anxious quest for security.

Cain and Abel provide us our first glimpse in Scripture of the devastating consequences of sibling rivalry. Scripture is replete with accounts of brothers who chose rivalry and competition rather than cooperation and communion. The stories are gripping—Jacob and Esau; Joseph and his brothers; Moses and Aaron; Abimelech (son of Gideon) and his brothers; the sons of David—the list seems endless. Rivalry and animosity among brothers does not cease with the Old

Testament. James and John jockey for prime seats in the kingdom of God, angering the other disciples. The parable we know best as the "prodigal son" is in reality a parable of *two* brothers. First John 3 raises the haunting absurdity of loving an *unseen* God while despising a *seen* brother. These narratives challenge us, for we live in a world that prizes and celebrates competition and rivalry. Our society argues that rivalry breeds courage, fortitude, drive, toughness, and independence. Scripture informs us that rivalry often begets animosity, jealousy, anger, envy, distance, and suspicion.

■ Is familial competition a good thing? Why or why not?
■ How does competition or rivalry relate to worship?

In a world given to celebrating winners and discarding losers, Scripture calls us to be our *brother's keeper*. Through God's challenge to Cain, we hear God challenging us to forego self-obsession and self-interest and love our brother! It is not without consequence that this act of anger occurs in relationship to worship. Tragically, it is often in our worship to God that we become most prone to competition that results in animosity. Misunderstanding the nature of our relationship with God, we begin to see worship as a place where we gain God's approval or disapproval. When God does not respond toward us the way we think he ought, we react with anger. In the New Testament, Jesus details the tragic ramifications that severed human relationships have upon worship. A right relationship with God is impossible when our relationships with each other are wrong.

> *"You have heard that it was said to those of ancient times, 'You shall not murder'; and 'whoever murders shall be liable to judgment.' But I say to you that if you are angry with a brother or sister, you will be liable to judgment; and if you insult a brother or sister, you will be liable to the council; and if you say, 'You fool,' you will be liable to the hell of fire. So when you are offering your gift at the altar, if you remember that your brother or sister has something against you, leave your gift there before the altar and go; first be reconciled to your brother or sister, and then come and offer your gift"* (Matthew 5:21-24).

■ What does choice have to do with our relationships with one another?

Genesis 4 reminds us of the importance of the choices we make. Though sin can be a powerful presence in our world and in our lives, it reminds us that we can choose *for* God and *for* our brother! We can choose to take responsibility for each other and "do well." We can choose to act rightly; by the grace of God we are capable of faithful living. We dare not minimize the choices—such choices are hard. Often, the hardest choice of all is the choice to reconcile with our brother! We do well to remind ourselves regularly of the deadly serious nature of sin, and that we are often most vulnerable to the power of sin when dealing with our "brother." We take comfort that as we make choices for our brother, so God makes choices *for* us! God's grace empowers us to empty ourselves of hatred and anger so that we might become our brother's keeper.

Genesis 6–9 brings us squarely into the presence of our God. These chapters powerfully testify that the God we worship is so fully engaged with his creation that he can be *hurt* by human sin. The flood confronts us not with a stern and distant judge, but with a grieving and pained parent. It is that divine sorrow and regret that makes the story so personal. We should not mistake the nature of the grief, however. God's sorrow is linked inseparably to his resolute commitment to bring his creation into line with his eternal purposes. Though God may impose eternal limitations upon himself (hanging up his bow in the sky), the flood does not nullify his promises or purposes. He wills to have us live in right relationship with him. The flood reminds us that God refuses to abandon his creation to its own self-destructive violence.

It is this God with whom we long to be in right relationship. Noah provides us wonderful guidance, for he is the first character in the Bible who has character. God declares Noah righteous. In Noah, we find the true meaning of righteousness. Noah lives responsibly before the Lord. He walks in accordance with the divine will. Significantly, Noah is the first person in the Bible who is *speechless* and *listens* to God! In contrast to Cain and his descendants, Noah "*heard God and did.*" He put himself under the guidance and direction of the Creator of the world. Noah *walks with God* (an expression used elsewhere only of Enoch and Abraham ["before God"]). Not surprisingly, his first act upon disembarking the ark is worship. For Noah, worship is an expression of gratitude (8:20), not a means to divine approval.

Out of the devastation of the flood, we encounter God's commitment to his creation articulated in covenant language. Genesis 6–9 shows us the heart of God; it is the heart of a promise keeper. God makes promises; his promises are eternal, they will need no renewing, only *remembering*. In Genesis 6–9 we encounter a faithful God who brings his creation back from the brink of chaos (triggered through human rebellion) and engages in re-creation. Seen through New Testament eyes, this God resonates powerfully with us. We meet here the God who promises to make all things new in a "new creation," who promises us that for anyone "in Christ, there is a new creation" (2 Corinthians 5:17). The present creation, battered and ravaged by human sin (Romans 8), will experience the gracious transformation of an all-powerful God who refuses to let sin and evil be the final word.

Just as Genesis 4 calls into question our current values about rivalry and competition, so Genesis 11 questions our contemporary obsessions with security and notoriety. In a world increasingly given to gated communities and seeking safety through separation, Genesis 11 reminds us that security comes not from a *place* but from a *person*! We are secure not because of *where* we live, but because of *with whom* we live. In like manner, fame comes not through self-promotion, but as a blessed gift from God. Such a vision redefines fame. In a world given to "making a name" for oneself, Genesis 11 reminds us that the "name" that really matters is the name God bestows upon us. Our lives take on significance against the backdrop of God's plan and purpose for our lives. Such will be the clear message of the sequel to the Tower of Babel—the Abraham narrative. Not surprisingly, the Tower of Babel episode is at times contrasted with the marvelous event at Pentecost in Acts 2.

- Explain the difference between worship out of gratitude and worship that seeks approval.
- What does it mean that God speaks his promises through covenant language?
- How do you define security? How can it be an obsession?

■ Contrast security and notoriety. How does God define these words?

In an environment where humans focus their efforts upon their own promotion and achievements, division and confusion often result. However, in an environment where the glorious deeds of the Lord are proclaimed, unity and understanding occur. The gospel is proclaimed; the word of God sounds forth clearly to all.

The earth will be affected more by divine faithfulness than by human sin. In both scenes humankind receives a blessing from God (1:28-30; 9:1). Both scenes entrust the animal realm to the care and protection of humankind (1:28-30; 2:18-20; 9:2-5). Perhaps most importantly, humanity after the flood is still created in the image of God (1:26; 9:6).

CHAPTER 5

Embracing the Call—
The Promise of Land

(Genesis 12–15)

enesis 12 transfers us into a new world. Genesis 1–11 recounts primeval history; Genesis 12–50 recounts patriarchal history. Where Genesis 1–11 surveys the entire landscape of creation, Genesis 12–50 narrows the focus. We now view the larger world of God's creation through the experiences of a particular segment of the earth's population. Genesis 12–50 traces the adventures of three of Israel's most prominent ancestors—Abraham, Jacob, and Joseph. Although numerous other figures will enter the drama, the bulk of the materials will concern these three patriarchs. To be overly simplistic, Genesis 12–25 narrates the journey of Abraham, Genesis 26–36 the struggles of Jacob, Genesis 37–50 the adventures of Joseph.

Numerous other players will cross the stage of this memorable production. As these patriarchs move throughout the earth, they will interact with a variety of peoples and cultures. The travelogue is extensive. Over the course of these several chapters we will spend time in Mesopotamia, Egypt, and numerous points in between. Just as a familiarity with the culture and worldview of the ancient Near East sheds light on Genesis 1–11, so archaeological discoveries of the past few centuries provide helpful insights into the period of the patriarchs.

Genesis 12–50 and the Ancient Near East

In recent years, biblical scholars have devoted considerable study to the patriarchal period and its relationship to the larger socio-historical world of the ancient Near East. Not surprisingly, dramatically divergent conclusions have been reached concerning the chronology and history of the period, and the significance of the archaeological evidence itself. Debate continues about the relation of various patriarchal practices to the social and legal practices of neighboring peoples.

Archaeological discoveries of the ancient Near East have greatly increased our knowledge of the larger world of the Bible. We have considerable information about the peoples and cultures surrounding ancient Israel. While significant gaps remain, excavation sites in Mesopotamia, Syria, Egypt, and Canaan have delivered a wealth of information. Though at times contested, these archaeological discoveries generally allow us to piece together a fairly coherent picture of the ancient Near Eastern world. It is important that we realize the function and *primary* value of archaeological evidence in relationship to the Bible. The primary value and purpose of archaeological discovery is not to prove or disprove the biblical record. Archaeological data *seldom* delivers conclusive proof or disproof. For this reason, archaeological data can be used by supporters of the Bible to confirm its historicity and by critics to deny the same! Rather, archaeological discoveries function best to *illuminate* the world of the Bible. These discoveries elucidate and shed light on the world in which the patriarchs lived and through which they traveled. It allows us to understand more precisely the nature of their journeys. It provides us insights into the social and cultural customs and mores of the time. We must remember that we are reading *family* narratives, and so it is not surprising that we do not encounter these families in the national histories of the ancient empires of the Near East. The socio-historical setting of the patriarchs is that of the early second millennium; their narratives reflect the world of the Middle Bronze Age.

A follow-up point needs stressing. As we read these narratives, we must always remember that a text of Scripture has *at least* two settings. The first setting involves the *occurrence* of the event being narrated. The second setting involves the *writing* of that event. In the Old Testament, we frequently encounter significant time gaps between events and the written recording of the events. Recognizing these gaps is not inconsequential. When a significant gap appears between when something occurred and when it was recorded in written form, the text often helps us by providing updates for place names or people that would have been unnecessary were there no time gap.

Issues of archaeology and history, while important and substantial, are not my primary focus. My interest lies elsewhere. I am primarily interested in the *theological* and *religious* message of these narratives. I believe the *principal* purpose for the recording of these narratives was to provide us a glimpse into the faith of our ancestors so that we might live faithful lives. As mentioned previously, these stories are narrated in such a way that we read them as *our* stories. They are not simply bland records of an ancient past, suitable only for nostalgic trips down memory lane. Rather, we realize as we read them that these stories throb with drama and passion. They grab us and refuse to let us go.

Journey provides the overarching metaphor for the patriarchal narratives. Journey says something significant about the life of faith and our relationship with God. Jacob spends considerable time *away from home*. In his return home, he must address his past, a past marked by unresolved conflict. Joseph spends his life in adverse circumstances. Throughout the patriarchal narratives, the concern for God's presence is ever present. If we read them as they were intended to be read, we realize we are often looking in a mirror. We see ourselves in these patriarchs.

Overview of Genesis 12–25

The Abraham narrative actually spans Genesis 11:27–25:18. The stories are captivating, interrelated, and deliver new insights with repeated readings. Numerous outlines have been suggested for this cycle of materials. To be overly simplistic, the promise to Abraham involves land and descendants. I have arbitrarily divided the materials into two major sections. In this chapter, we will view the promise as it relates to the promise of land. In the following chapter, we will view the promise as it relates to the promise of descendants. In this chapter, we will view the relationship between God and Abraham through the *eyes of God*. In the following chapter, we will view the relationship between God and Abraham through the *eyes of Abraham*. Not surprisingly, these categories are not airtight and so some spillover will occur.

When reading narrative materials, we must be careful not to miss the forest for the trees. As we move from story to story, an awareness of the larger structure and development of the narrative keeps us focused. The function of one section of the narrative often is determined by its setting in the larger narrative. Because of this, a sense of the structure and outline of the narrative is helpful. As mentioned above, one approach to the Abraham narrative focuses upon the central feature of the promise to Abraham, a promise consisting principally of land and descendants. Securing the land dominates at the outset (Genesis 12–15); the land gives way to securing descendants as the narrative progresses (Genesis 15–22). Key narrative elements come in pairs! We have two genealogical notations (11:10-32; 25:1-18); two references to the "old country" (11:27-32; 24); two accounts where Abraham endangers his wife Sarah (12:10-20; 20:1-18); two accounts where Abraham rescues Lot (13–14; 18:16–19:38); two incidents involving Hagar and Ishmael (16; 21:8-21); two narratives detailing the birth of Isaac (18:1-15; 21:1-7); two interactions with the Philistine king Abimelech (20; 21:22-34); and two testings of Abraham that involve a journey (12:1-9; 22:1-19).

Like earlier narratives in Genesis 1–11 the Abraham narrative may reflect chiasm or ring composition. This feature appears throughout Scripture. The biblical writers knew that an effective way to communicate memorably God's word was to present the second half of the narrative in reverse order from the first half. The following outline (Outline 3) suggests such a possibility:

OUTLINE 3 ■

(A) An introductory genealogy (11:10-32)

  (B) Abraham migrates from Haran and separates from Nahor ([12:1-3], 12:4-5)

   (C) Abraham builds altars and is promised land (12:5b-9 [13:14-18])

    (D) Abraham endangers Sarai, his "wife-sister" (12:10-20)

     (E) Abraham makes a border agreement with Lot (13:1-13)

      (F) Foreign kings defeat Sodom; Lot is rescued (14:1-24)

       (G) God confirms his covenant through sacrifice (15:1-21)

        (H) Hagar is expelled and rescued (16:1-16)

       (G) Abraham confirms the covenant through circumcision (17:1-27)

      (F) God destroys Sodom; Lot is rescued (18:1–19:38)

     (E) Abraham makes a border agreement with Abimelech (21:22-34)

    (D) Abraham endangers Sarah, his "wife-sister" (20:1-18)

   (C) Abraham builds an altar (22:6) and land is secured (22:17b; 23:1-20)

  (B) Abraham sends Eliezer to Haran and reunites with Nahor's line (24:1-67)

(A) A concluding genealogy (22:20-24; 25:1-18)

The major themes of the narrative are present from the opening scene—journey, promise, choice, land, descendants, infertility, extended family, divine will, and human responsibility.

Entrance into and Exit from the Promised Land (11:27–12:20)

The transition from Genesis 11 to 12 is striking and momentous. We watch as the inhabitants of the land wander away from their tower and city to various parts of the earth. They depart having failed to secure the lasting fame they sought. Their unfinished tower and city stand as silent monuments to their presumptuousness and anxiety. As we read, their insecurity becomes ours. What does this divine response mean for humankind? Will humanity be doomed to wander aimlessly, making its way anxiously across a foreboding and forbidding landscape? Has God finally decided not to start over? Will there be no renewal this time?

Genesis 12 resolutely answers these fretful questions. God refuses to abandon his creatures to their own devices. He desires to bless his creation, his human creatures in particular. He begins again, but this time in a dramatically different fashion. He selects a human representative as his agent of blessing. Through Abram, God will bless humankind.

The conclusion of Genesis 11 offers us our first glimpse at the principal character in the next narrative. It provides us a genealogical overview of the family of Abram. We meet Abram's father (Terah), his brothers (Nahor and Haran), and their several wives (Sarai, Milcah). The genealogical data provides us the information necessary to make sense of the following scenes. Abram will take responsibility for his nephew Lot, whose father Haran dies early. Strikingly, in a genealogy given to documenting sons and daughters, Sarai *the wife* is defined by her barrenness! Lot's lack of a father and Sarai's lack of a child will figure prominently in the ensuing narratives.

As Genesis 12 opens, we hear God calling Abram to depart from his native land and journey westward. The directive surprises us, for we have just read of his move in the preceding genealogy. However, we realize that the move is incomplete! Abram, originally from Ur, a city in southern Mesopotamia, journeyed with his extended family northward to the old Hurrian city of Haran, and apparently settled there. Time has passed. God now calls Abram to repack and continue the journey. For God, Haran is simply a transitional stage in the journey; it is not the final destination. Given our knowledge of the ancient Near East, we are left to speculate for the stop at Haran. Scholars often suggest that Haran was a comfortable place for a family from Ur. Although geographically some distance from Ur, Haran may have had similar customs and a similar religious worldview. The evidence suggests that both Ur and Haran gave prominence to worship of the moon god.

Genesis 12:1-3 provides the theological center for the book of Genesis (and perhaps the entire Pentateuch):

> *Now the LORD said to Abram, "Go from your country and your kindred and your father's house to the land that I will show you. I will make of you a great nation, and I will bless you, and make your name great, so that you will be a blessing. I will bless those who bless you, and the one who curses you I will curse; and in you all the families of the earth shall be blessed."*

The response to God's call is succinct—*"Abram went, as the LORD had told him; and Lot went with him."* Having already left his homeland, he now leaves his kindred. The course of human history changes forever in the response Abram makes to these three short verses. Genesis 12:1-3 contains promises and charges. God promises Abram that he will become a great nation; in striking contrast to the *nameless* builders of Babel, God will bestow upon him a great name. Not only will Abram be blessed, but also in him the rest of humanity will find its blessing.

God calls Abram to embrace the promise. However, to receive the promise, he must abandon his past. The moment is poignant. While the people of Babel may wander aimlessly, Abram will wander with a purpose. This is not a scattering; Abram is called to "move to the land I will show you." His security will not be realized in a settled location; he will move throughout the land that God has promised him. Most importantly, Abram is called not to obey a command, but to *embrace a promise*. We dare not move too quickly past this moment. At the beginning of Genesis, God created Adam and gave his life meaning through vocation. He entrusted Adam with the care and oversight of the garden. More broadly, he gave all humanity responsibility for the care and maintenance of the earth. Now, God entrusts to Abram a pivotal vocation for the rest of humanity. Abram is blessed, but *blessed for a purpose!* As he moves throughout the land, God commissions him to bestow blessing upon those he meets. The nature of his encounters will determine whether blessing or cursing results. If we read the narrative as if reading for the first time, we cannot help but wonder whether God's purpose for Abram will take a route similar to that of Adam (and earlier humankind) or whether the route will more faithfully track the divine intent.

Viewed from another angle, we should remind ourselves that the promise to Abram is neither neat nor tidy. Regarding the promise of numerous descendants, the text has already informed us that Sarai his wife is barren. Regarding the promise of land, the text will shortly inform us that this "promised land" already contains inhabitants.

If Abram followed the traditional caravan routes of the time, he would have journeyed west to Carchemish, turned south to Aleppo, on to Damascus, until he reached Shechem. The text states the obvious—Abram is not a native to this new land—*"at that time the Canaanites were in the land"* (v. 6). Canaanite is not an ethnic designation; it is a social designation. This new land Abram enters is comprised of numerous ethnic groups and peoples. They are Canaanite in that they share a common feature—they engage in commerce. (The term Canaanite means "trader, trafficker.")

Genesis 12:4-9 recounts Abram's movements throughout the land of Canaan. Two aspects merit comment. First, Abram moves from place to place for theological reasons. As he makes his stops, he engages in a most significant activity—he builds an altar. Although we likely move quickly through these texts, this act of worship is laden with meaning. In the ancient world, building an altar to one's god was an external demonstration of allegiance to that god and a declaration that the territory the altar encompassed belonged to the god worshiped. Appropriately, at his first stop near Shechem, God reaffirms that Abram's descendants will inhabit the place. Abram builds an altar. When he later relocates between Bethel and Ai, Abram builds an altar and worships God—he invokes the name of the Lord. Abram is faithfully claiming this already occupied land for his God.

Second, from a socio-historical perspective, we should be clear regarding the nature of Abram's (and his successors) migrations. Abram does not live the life of a Bedouin nomad. That is, we should not envision Abram daily rolling up his bedroll and loading the tent on the wagon. Abram is a pastoral nomad. He has flocks of sheep and herds of goats. In this desert environment, he moves as the climate and pastureland dictate. Abram's pastoral lifestyle will figure prominently in subsequent narratives.

Abram is no sooner settled securely in the land of promise than famine breaks out! He enters the land from the north only to slide out the south. Again, knowledge of the ancient Near East helps us. Canaan was a land heavily dependent upon rainfall. Largely semi-arid, it suffered greatly during times of drought. Famine was a constant concern. In contrast, Egypt was a land dominated not by rain (it received none!), but by the Nile. Annually the Nile overflowed its banks, dispensing valuable topsoil for farming. Through irrigation, the Nile offered a constant source of life-giving water. During times of drought and famine, the inhabitants of Canaan typically made their way to Egypt for survival.

Genesis 12:10-20 provides us our first scene of the promise jeopardized. We cannot help but wonder whether Abram doubts God's ability to bless and protect him beyond the borders of the promised land. (In the ancient Near East, many people thought a god's power and protection was limited to a particular region.) Abram comes from a polytheistic background. Does he question whether his God of promise can deliver from any location? Does he, like his Mesopotamian ancestors, assume this God who has chosen him can only protect him inside the borders of Canaan? Whatever the motivation, Abram initiates a plan of self-protection. In a world of power imbalance and social inequity, Abram assumes danger lies ahead. He considers Egypt a land where husbands of beautiful women are killed so that they can be incorporated into the royal harem. Husbands of beautiful women may fare poorly, but surely not brothers!

The ensuing scene is noteworthy. True to his suspicions, the royal servants recognize and relate the beauty of Sarai to the Pharaoh. Their praise of Sarai results in Abram receiving blessing. However, it is the *Pharaoh* who blesses him, not *God!* Pharaoh supplies Abram with livestock and servants. Amazingly, in return for his treatment of Abram, the Pharaoh receives not a blessing, but affliction! He suffers greatly. (A later rabbinic Midrash considered the plague inflicted on Pharaoh to be impotence!) When the Pharaoh discovers that Sarai is more accurately Abram's wife than sister, he lectures Abram! The moment is dramatic:

> *So Pharaoh called Abram, and said, "What is this you have*
> *done to me? Why did you not tell me that she was your wife?*
> *Why did you say, 'She is my sister,' so that I took her for my wife?*
> *Now then, here is your wife, take her, and be gone"* (12:18-19).

Pharaoh instructs his servants to send Abram and his belongings out of the country.

The scene is memorable, and intricately told. Ironically, Abram *lies to protect the promise*, but the Pharaoh *takes the promise out of Abram's hand!* Abram is enriched, but enriched by a foreign king. To protect himself, Abram jeopardizes his wife. In return, he is enriched because of the wife he endangered! God's original intent for a husband and wife (Genesis 2:22-24) escapes Abram's vision. If Abram questions God's ability to provide protection and blessing beyond the borders of the promised land, he similarly may yet have to learn the *true source* of his blessings.

God's will to realize his purposes through Abram overshadows the entire scene. Abram's journey of faith is only beginning; he has much to learn about the God who has called him and promised to bless him. Abram's actions have brought Egypt close to curse rather than blessing. However, the promises are intact, for the story is more about the nature of a powerfully faithful God than a fragile and fickle human.

Abram and Lot—Separation (Genesis 13)

Abram travels northward with his entourage and re-enters the land of promise. He makes his way through the southern desert of the Negeb until he arrives again at his earlier encampment near Bethel. God is faithful to his promises. Though Abram may yet need instruction in how he will be a blessing, God is moving forward in blessing Abram. The flocks of Abram and his nephew Lot are expanding so rapidly that the immediate pastureland cannot support them. Strife among the shepherds breaks out.

Abram addresses the problem. Perhaps having learned valuable lessons in Egypt, he now entrusts himself fully to God's care. Abram calls Lot and offers him first choice of pasturage. Lot lifts his eyes and scans the horizon. In one direction lies flat and fertile grassland. In the other direction rises the rugged and ragged hill country. Lot makes what seems an obvious choice. His flocks will flourish in the former environment; his life will go smoothly in such terrain. When Lot departs, God invites Abram to "lift his eyes" toward the seemingly unforgiving terrain Lot has left him. While Abram scans the horizon, God reiterates and elaborates his previous promise to Abram. God calls Abram to envision these hills populated with his descendants, descendants so numerous they will cover the land like dust! Lot moves southward and pitches his tent near the urban sprawl of Sodom; Abram moves toward Hebron, but pitches his tent at the oaks of Mamre, and builds another altar.

For those of us who know the sequel, this opening narrative between Abram and Lot carries added meaning. Abram reverses his behavior in Egypt; here he fully trusts in the promises of God. Having experienced God's powerful will to bless and protect him, he knows he can let Lot take whatever land he desires. God's ability to bless is not limited by location! Where Lot lifts his eyes and chooses for himself, Abram waits for God to lift his eyes and reveal to Abram his plan. The Lord promises Abram this land will remain "forever"; Lot's choice of land will soon suffer destruction.

Abram and Lot—Recovery (Genesis 14)

Genesis 14 depicts the tragic consequences of Lot's land choice. The first part of the narrative echoes the language of ancient Near Eastern military campaign annals. The text several times explains places that may be unfamiliar to later readers (note the parentheses in vv. 2,3,7,8,17). A coalition of eastern kings traverses what is later known as the "King's Highway" to squelch a rebellion in the west. The rebel kings are summarily routed in a series of sweeping campaigns. The conquering coalition gathers up the riches from the abandoned cities and heads home. Lot is caught up in the sweep. When Abram hears of Lot's kidnapping, he assembles a contingent of soldiers from his own house (318 men—Abram is truly blessed!) and heads northward to rescue Lot. He attacks the coalition at night and retrieves his nephew Lot, as well as a substantial portion of the goods taken by the departing kings.

The scene that captures our imagination is the final scene. Upon his return to the southland, the surviving king of Sodom and the king of Salem greet Abram. King Melchizedek of Salem (=Jerusalem? [see Psalm 76:3]), also a priest, brings bread and wine for the occasion. In a memorable scene, Melchizedek blesses Abram:

> *"Blessed be Abram by God Most High [El Elyon], maker of heaven and earth; and blessed be God Most High [El Elyon], who has delivered your enemies into your hand!"*
>
> *And Abram gave him one tenth of everything. Then the king of Sodom said to Abram, "Give me the persons, but take the goods for yourself." But Abram said to the king of Sodom, "I have sworn to the* LORD, **God Most High** *[Yahweh, El Elyon], maker of heaven and earth, that I would not take a thread or sandal-thong or anything that is yours,* **so that you might not say, 'I have made Abram rich.'** *I will take nothing but what the young men have eaten, and the share of the men who went with me. . . ."* (14:19-24, emphasis added).

Abram has learned the lesson of Egypt well. His riches come from the Lord, not an earthly king! In striking contrast to the episode in Egypt, where Abram left *indebted* to the Pharaoh, the kings of Canaan now find themselves *indebted* to Abram. Abram also makes sure everyone present knows the correct identification of the Most High (El Elyon) Creator of the universe—it is none other than the God of his promise and call—Yahweh! (Yahweh is the personal name for God in the Old Testament, in earlier translations mistakenly vocalized Jehovah.)

The Covenant Is Revisited— God Fully Commits (Genesis 15)

Abram, surely energized with his successful sortie against these eastern kings, must consider the land portion of the promise secure. Altars he has built to the Lord stand strategically throughout the land, confirming the divine promise. However, the promise of land is only half the promise. In Genesis 15 we overhear Abram question the descendant portion of the promise. God may be his "shield" (*magen*), and his "reward" (*sakar*) may be great, but it is of limited value if he has no heir on whom he can bestow it. God's promise of descendants beyond counting comes up against Abram's inability to produce a single heir!

Genesis 15 links closely with the preceding events in Genesis 14 (Melchizedek) and the following episode in Genesis 16 (Hagar). At the close of chapter 14, Abram rightly declines any *reward* from the king of Sodom, so that no one can suggest that his riches come from any source other than the Lord. In Genesis 15, God promises Abram a reward far beyond his imagination. However, in Genesis 16 Abram again takes matters into his own hand and attempts to assist God in providing an heir (Ishmael). (In Genesis 15 Abram argues that his slave Eliezer is his only viable heir; in Genesis 16 he attempts to help God by siring a child through Sarai's slave Hagar.) The Lord refuses Abram's help and dissension rather than blessing surface in Abram's house.

Internally, Genesis 15 divides neatly into two somewhat parallel panels: vv. 1-6; vv. 7-21. This chapter returns us to the two elements of the promise God made to Abram in Genesis 12—descendants and land. The first section addresses the issue of *gift*. In response to the Lord's offer of a reward, Abram asks, *"O LORD God, what will you give me, for I continue childless?"* The second section addresses the issue of *knowledge*. In response to God's promise of land, Abram asks, *"O LORD God, how am I to know that I shall possess it?"*

In the first scene of Genesis 15, Abram tries to help the Lord fulfill the descendant portion of the promise. Familiar with the customs of the times for childless couples, he moves in a predictable manner. He puts forth his chief servant Eliezer as a suitable heir. Through Abram's adoption of Eliezer, God can realize his promise! To Abram's suggestion, God responds verbally and dramatically.

God first reiterates the promise made in chapter 12. When Abram questions the viability of this promise, God responds unequivocally with a dramatic enactment. The final scene is simultaneously meaningful and incredibly enigmatic. God instructs Abram to gather a variety of sacrificial animals and birds. The animals are halved. At dusk, Abram falls into a deep sleep, a sleep like the one experienced by Adam prior to his surgery. Abram's sleep is fitful rather than restful, for it is accompanied by a terrifying darkness. In contrast to vv. 1-6, where the divine act responding to Abram's request for a gift involves an awake and alert Abram viewing the brightness of the stars at night, here the divine act responding to Abram's request for knowledge involves a sleeping Abram engulfed by a terrifying darkness. The deep sleep and the terrifying darkness may capture the dual nature of the divine message that Abram receives. On the one hand, God once again promises Abram that he will faithfully fulfill his promise and give Abram numerous offspring. However, the road ahead for those descendants will be

EMBRAC

neither smooth nor straight. Ominous trials awa
experience loss of the land and grueling slavery
Though unidentified, the land of Egypt is clearl
just as the final word in Genesis 1–11 was con
rather than punishment, so Abram's descendant
return to the land God has given the patriarch and

In the final scene, Abram sees a smoking pot and flaming torch pass between the halved animals. The text simply concludes, *"on that day the LORD made a covenant with Abram."* (In Hebrew the expression "to make a covenant" is literally "to cut a covenant.") Though enigmatic, I would suggest the following interpretation. In the ancient Near East, there is some evidence that covenant ceremonies at times concluded with a symbolic sacrificial act. In that ceremony, animals were cut in half and the participants walked between the halves. The intent of the symbolic act seems obvious—the participants declared through this act that they should be so treated (halved) should they fail to honor the covenant agreement. (We have such evidence at the town of Mari in north Syria; mention is also made in the Aramaic treaties of Sefire. Our only biblical attestation of such activity is in Jeremiah 34:18-20.) In Genesis 15, God passes between the halved animals. If such is a correct reading, the theological message is almost overwhelming. The God we worship commits himself so fully to Abram that he willingly puts his life on the line should he not keep his promise to Abram! The King and Lord of the universe freely and without hesitation gives himself to Abram.

Finding Ourselves in Genesis 12–15

If we read Genesis 12–15 with open eyes and listen with attentive ears, we cannot fail to hear God's word to us. We realize as we move from scene to scene that Abram's story is *our* story! The landscape may look different and the cultural norms sound strange, but the vision of a faithful and persistent God and the diverse responses of Abram resonate with our own life stories. As we read, we recognize in Abram's faith journey our own journey of faith. We find in Abram's better and worse responses our own moments of genuine faith and periods of feeble doubt. Like Abram, we at times manifest faith and at other times manifest fear.

■ List your moments of genuine faith and feeble doubt.

These opening chapters of the Abram narrative testify to a faithful God who tirelessly pursues his promises. Though Genesis 12 may document a *strategic* change on the part of God in dealing with humankind, it quickly confirms that no *character* change has occurred! The God who created the universe and repeatedly renewed his creation now wills to bless that creation through the life of Abram. Never is the divine commitment to humanity more evident than in Genesis 15. The God we worship is not a God who sits aloof and distant from his creatures. He is a God who willingly makes himself vulnerable to us. It is worthy of note that the Lord acknowledges his undivided allegiance to his promise not merely through speech, but through action as well. God demonstrates his commitment through a ritual "death-defying" act. As Christians, when we read Genesis 15 our minds cannot help but race forward to the New Testament affirmation of God's total vulnerability at the cross.

Abram exhibits for us the contours of a life of faith. In faith, he leaves the security of known surroundings and family and journeys forth to an undisclosed (to him) location. In faith he repeatedly embraces the promise as he erects altars along the way. With each altar he claims this land for his promising God. In faith he allows Lot first choice, knowing that his God can provide plenty out of any environment. In faith he declares that his God will provide for him; he will not allow others to take credit for enriching him (so Genesis 14). He willingly and without hesitation ventures forth to rescue Lot, a nephew who lives with a different vision. However, making faithful decisions is not always easy. Difficult circumstances often hinder our vision. With clouded vision, we often respond with fear rather than faith. Abram operates more from fear than faith when he enters Egypt. Like Abram, we may at times wonder whether God is present with us as we move from place to place. Following the immediate success of a campaign, Abram questions out loud God's ability to provide an heir (Genesis 15). It is most noteworthy that in the very midst of Abram's questioning we read these words: *"And he believed the LORD; and the LORD reckoned it to him as righteousness"* (15:6).

- Is it wrong to question God? Why or why not?
- Give an example where circumstances clouded your vision of faith.

The language is significant. Abram is *reckoned* righteous, not *declared* righteous. The reckoning is rooted in his faith. This text provides us with a powerful example of biblical righteousness. Righteousness is primarily a term of relationship, not a moral designation. It designates the nature of the relationship between two persons. *God pronounces his relationship with Abram "right" because Abram has embraced the call.* He has left land and kin to embark on this journey of faith. Though at times he struggles with the delay in the fulfillment of the promise, Abram never abandons the call. Such a vision of righteousness can empower us today. The "rightness" of our relationship with God is rooted not in our moral perfection (since "all have sinned and fall short of the glory of God"). Rather, it results from our embracing God's call and claim upon our lives. God's promise(s) always involves human responsibility (call). God wills to be Lord of our lives. As we embrace that call and lay claim to his promises, we experience a right relationship. Such an act is "faith." This Old Testament understanding of faith matches well with the vision of faith we encounter in the gospel. Repeatedly, Jesus heals and blesses people because of their faith. In the Gospels, faith is less assent to intellectual propositions or an inner disposition of the heart and more an outward action rooted in the conviction that the one promising can and will effect the promise. Simply put, the faith of those people is recognizing in Jesus the presence of God and *acting upon that recognition.* They see in Jesus the promise of God made flesh and act. Like Abram, they experience God's blessing and embrace—their *faith saves them.* In contrast, *fear* involves taking matters into our own hands; doubting that God has the power to accomplish his promises, we attempt to "help" God through our own endeavors. Interestingly, such actions typically result in bringing "curse" rather than blessing and pose dangerous threats to the promise.

Fittingly, the New Testament writers found in Genesis 15:6 rich resources for explicating the appropriate response to a promise-keeping God (Romans 4:3,20-24; Galatians 3:6; James 2:23). Belief involves fixing one's eyes on the promise keeper who freely and willingly commits himself fully to his creation and his covenant people. When Abram *acknowledges the nature of God*, he receives divine affirmation of the rightness of his relationship. Our "righteousness" is rooted first and foremost in our acknowledgment of the essential nature of God. As we acknowledge God's nature as promise keeper and faithful giver, our own actions are transformed. Based on Genesis 15, one clear implication of this right belief is that we now take a long-range view toward life. Although the immediate horizon may appear tenuous and fraught with difficulties (e.g., v. 13), we know for certain that the promises of God stand, for they are rooted in a God who has fully committed himself to us and to our well-being. Such an acknowledgment transforms our present, for now the present circumstances pale as our vision of the very nature of God comes to dominate our horizon. When we capture this vision, God reckons us righteous. Capturing such a vision answers Abram's and our request for a gift and for knowledge.

■ How does a long-range view of life help us to cope with the present challenges to our faith?

Finally, these opening chapters remind us that our life with God is a pilgrimage. Such a reminder may be comforting and discomforting at the same time. In a world in constant flux, we take comfort that the God who faithfully travels with Abram promises the same presence to the children of Abram. In a world plagued by loneliness, we affirm we are never alone. The Maker of heaven and earth freely and fully gives himself to us. However, the motif of pilgrimage may cause some discomfort. Although we have pilgrimage at the heart of our narrative as Americans, for us pilgrimage is typically a *temporary circumstance* to maneuver on the way to settlement! We must proceed with extreme caution as children of God. If we listen faithfully, Scripture reminds us that this world is not our final destination; pilgrimage is not a temporary circumstance to overcome. Like Abram, we live as pilgrims on a journey. God calls us to *live light* in this world, to travel in such a manner that we never lose sight of our *primary* purpose in this world. As Abram's children, we live to bestow God's blessing upon the rest of humankind. As we journey throughout our world, we bring God's blessing to a world in desperate need.

Like faith and fear, we must define *blessing* biblically. Blessing in Genesis has nothing to do with a sentimental wish for happiness or a pious way to say good-bye. Blessing involves matters of life and death. It encompasses God's gifts of power and vitality, his offer of meaningful and abundant life. In Genesis 1 God blesses the birds and fish (day 5), humanity (day 6) and the Sabbath (day 7). Blessing closely links with fertility (fruitfulness) and multiplication (abundance). In Genesis 12, God promises Abram the same blessings of meaningful and abundant life. However, this does not conclude the story. Divine blessings are for sharing. God calls Abram to a life of pilgrimage so that he might bestow blessings on the rest of humanity. As Abram embraces the promises of God, he bestows blessing on those with whom he comes in contact.

In a world obsessed with receiving blessings, we declare that our primary purpose is to *give* blessing. The church desperately needs to hear afresh the word of the Lord proclaimed through Abram. To believers enamored with receiving God's blessings in their own lives, we declare that God calls us to dispense God's blessings to others. Like Abram, his descendants live to share the wonderful blessings of God to a world in need and wandering aimlessly.

■ In what ways can knowing that life is a pilgrimage be both comforting and discomforting?
■ How do we dispense God's blessings to others?

As mentioned earlier, these narratives are written in such a manner that they call us to join our story with Abram's story. The New Testament writers clearly affirm such a perspective. In a most remarkable passage, Paul states:

And if you belong to Christ, then you are Abram's offspring, heirs according to the promise (Galatians 3:29).

Hebrews 11:8-16 makes clear that our story of faith is inextricably tied to that of Abram. In Abram we find our paradigm for pilgrimage, faith, and right relationship with God. In Abram we encounter one who prefigures for us the promise of Jesus:

"And everyone who has left houses or brothers or sisters or father or mother or children or fields, for my name's sake, will receive a hundredfold, and will inherit eternal life" (Matthew 19:29).

In a world obsessed with receiving blessings, we declare that our primary purpose is to give blessing. The church desperately needs to hear afresh the word of the Lord proclaimed through Abram. To believers enamored with receiving God's blessings in their own lives, we declare that God calls us to dispense God's blessings to others. Like Abram, his descendants live to share the wonderful blessings of God to a world in need and wandering aimlessly.

CHAPTER 6

Embracing The Call—The Promise of Descendants
(Genesis 16–23)

A well-known line captures the essence of the patriarchal narratives—"history never looks like history when you're living through it." The narratives of Abraham, Isaac, Jacob, and Joseph exhibit countless twists and turns, potential wrong endings, and ambiguities. We read each narrative scene with anticipation, thinking we have successfully maneuvered a crisis, only to find another roadblock in the road ahead.

Such is the case in the Abraham narrative. The twin promises of land and descendants constantly loom as a problem to be solved. In the early chapters of Abraham's life, we watch Abraham enter the Promised Land only to exit during a famine. Abraham will make his way faithfully through this land, rescuing relatives and "making a name" for himself with the local rulers. True to the promise, he will be a blessing to those in this land (Genesis 14).

However, we know the promise has two components—land . . . and descendants. Genesis 15 provides us a glimpse of Abraham's first endeavor to help God resolve the lack of descendants. To his suggestion that his servant Eliezer function as heir, God responds with "fear not, I am your shield." In Genesis 16–22, the issue of descendants takes center stage. Abraham has been in the land for a decade with an heir no closer in sight than when he entered the land. He hears the promise, but surely must wonder about its timing!

The Covenant Circumvented (Genesis 16)

Genesis 16 details Sarai's attempt to provide Abram with descendants. Still unable to bear a child, she offers her slave-girl Hagar as a surrogate mother. This is our first knowledge of Hagar. The rabbis speculated, possibly correctly, that Hagar was a gift the Pharaoh gave Sarai at her exit from Egypt. Since Sarai cannot produce a child, she invokes a custom of the time and suggests Abram have a child through her slave-girl. In reverse fashion, the language echoes later male levirate marriage language (see Deuteronomy 25:5-10). Ten years have passed since entering the land, Sarai remains barren, and so Abram *listens to the voice of his wife*. (We remember an earlier time when Adam *listened to the voice of his wife*, rather than to God's voice.) Abram conceives a child with Hagar. The ensuing scene is memorable.

> *He went in to Hagar, and she conceived; and when she saw that she had conceived, she looked with contempt on her mistress. Then Sarai said to Abram, "May the wrong done to me be on you! I gave my slave-girl to your embrace, and when she saw that she had conceived, she looked on me with contempt. May the LORD judge between you and me! But Abram said to Sarai, "Your slave-girl is in your power; do to her as you please." Then Sarai dealt harshly with her, and she ran way from her* (16:4-6).

The conception brings not joy to the family, but bitterness and tension. In fact, the term *contempt* derives from the same root as the word for *curse* (*qll*). The blessing the promise intended has resulted in curse. Sarai's response fascinates us. When Abram called her to engage in duplicity in Egypt and allowed her to enter Pharaoh's house, Sarai was strangely silent. Now, following this episode, she becomes vocal, blames Abram for her troubles, and abuses Hagar. (The abuse Sarai gives Hagar will be the same term used later for the abuse the Egyptians give the Hebrew slaves in Egypt. The line literally reads—*Sarai oppressed her*.) Attempting to help God fulfill his promises has not resulted in blessing for the household of Abram.

Hagar flees the intolerable situation. Though separating herself from the *bearer* of the promise and heading home to Egypt, she is not separated from the *giver* of the promise. Though Hagar will not carry the promise of Abram, she will experience the blessing. Curse will not be the final chapter of this story, but blessing. A messenger from the Lord informs Hagar that her offspring will be multitudinous. God has paid heed ("heard") to her affliction; her firstborn will be named Ishmael ("God hears"). However, the message carries mixed news. This child will live a tumultuous life. Conflict will be the nature of his existence. The angel of the Lord instructs her to return to Sarai's house and submit to her mistress. Hagar submits to the divine instructions. Before leaving, she designates God "El-Roi" ("God of my seeing?") and the place Beer-lehai-roi ("Well of the Living One who sees me"). The place is near Kadesh (about 45 miles southwest of Beersheba).

The Covenant Embraced (Genesis 17)

If Genesis 16 depicts the nature of Abram's life when he distances himself from the covenant, Genesis 17 opens a window into his life when the covenant is fully embraced. In many ways, Genesis 17 functions as the human counterpart to God's total commitment to Abram in Genesis 15. Just as God demonstrates his complete commitment to Abram in the ritual act in Genesis 15, so now he calls Abram to engage in a ritual act to manifest his absolute embrace of the promises made to him.

Genesis 17 falls neatly into four sections. The chapter opens with God reaffirming his promise to Abram of numerous descendants (vv. 1-8); it follows with a call to Abraham to demonstrate his commitment to this promise through the act of circumcision (vv. 9-14); God next affirms that the promised descendants will come from Sarah (vv. 15-22); the scene closes with Abraham carrying out the divine instructions (vv. 23-27). Throughout the scene word-plays mark key moments, most notably through the changing of the names of key figures.

Thirteen years have elapsed between the close of Genesis 16 and the opening of Genesis 17. Abram, 86 when Ishmael was born, is now 99. If the promise of descendants seems distant after ten years in the land, surely it seemed forgotten at the beginning of Genesis 17! God appears to Abram and reaffirms his promise. Abram will become the ancestor of a multitude of nations. Such a declaration must have seemed strange to a father of a single child by surrogate parenthood! In Genesis 1, God called upon his first human creatures to *"be fruitful and multiply, to fill the earth."* He now declares to Abram that He will make the childless patriarch exceedingly fruitful. Just as he made a promise to Noah never to flood the earth again, so now he promises Abram the land of Canaan as an everlasting holding. To capture this dramatic moment, God changes the name of his promise bearer—Abram ("exalted father") will become Abraham ("father of a multitude"). At the same time, God provides Abraham with a new name by which to know his God who will make all this happen—*El Shaddai* ("God Almighty"). (This designation for God will mark pivotal moments throughout the remainder of Genesis.)

God now calls Abraham to fully commit. He calls upon Abraham to manifest his complete allegiance to this promising

God through the ritual of circumcision. Just as the rainbow in the sky was a sign of God's commitment to lovingly care for his creation, so now he calls upon Abraham to embrace fully the call to live in right relationship with this same God. Circumcision will become the quintessential confessional act for Abraham and his descendants! The commitment must be total. Anyone—native, foreigner, slave, free—who declares an intention to live within the promise of Abraham's orbit must submit to circumcision.

God repeats his promise of numerous descendants, bringing Sarai once again to center stage. Like Abraham, she also receives a new name—Sarai > Sarah (dialectical variants of "princess"). This "princess" will become the mother of "nations and kings of peoples." Abraham's response captures the twenty-three years of living with this promise:

> *Then Abraham fell on his face and laughed, and said to himself, "Can a child be born to a man who is a hundred years old? Can Sarah, who is ninety years old, bear a child?" And Abraham said to God, "O that Ishmael might live in your sight!"* (17:17-18).

We cannot help but wonder in which direction Abraham will proceed. Will he let 23 years of non-fulfillment of this portion of the promise dictate his next move, or will he embrace the promise? At this stage, uncertainty remains. On the one hand, Abraham asks God to revisit his position on Ishmael, for here is a flesh and blood descendant. On the other hand, he calls his wife Sarah (her new name), not Sarai.

As the chapter closes, God addresses the question of Ishmael while Abraham clarifies for us his commitment to the promise. God declares that Ishmael will not carry Abraham's promise, but will bear Abraham's blessing. The Lord responds:

> *As for Ishmael, I have heard you; I will bless him and make him fruitful and exceedingly numerous; he shall be the father of twelve princes, and I will make him a great nation. But my covenant I will establish with Isaac, whom Sarah shall bear to you at this season next year"* (17:20-21).

Abraham engages. He takes his son Ishmael and the remainder of his household and circumcises them. God manifested his total commitment to Abraham in Genesis 15; Abraham now reciprocates with an act of total commitment in Genesis 17. God's call at the beginning of Genesis 17—"walk before me and be blameless"—Abraham embraces. The language is royal language (see 1 Kings 3:6; 9:4; 2 Kings 20:3), language fitting for one who will become the father of kings. The Lord calls Abraham to live, always conscious of God's constant presence and in complete surrender to that presence (such is the meaning of "blameless").

Divine Visitors (Genesis 18–19)

Genesis 18–19 continues the concern for Abraham's descendants. As the narrative opens, three travelers approach Abraham's tent in the heat of the afternoon (18:1-8). Abraham initially is unaware of the special nature of his visitors. Only subsequently will he learn their identity (18:9-15). God, one of the three visitors, determines to divulge his plan of destruction to his covenant partner Abraham. A discussion of the justice of such an action ensues between Abraham and God (18:16-33). Genesis 19 recounts the destruction of Sodom and Gomorrah and the narrow escape of Lot and his daughters.

In ancient Israel, hospitality functioned as a principal virtue. Visitors were to be accorded hospitality as they traveled from place to place. Outsiders were provided shelter and lodging at evening. In an environment hostile to travelers at night, the resident host provided respite and protection. Hospitality to a stranger demonstrated a most basic form of human righteousness—the right treatment of another human being.

Abraham manifests extraordinary hospitality. He is generous to a fault. He offers the best of his pantry—the choicest flour and prime beef. He supplements the lavish meal with the everyday staples of cream and curds. In deference to his guests, while they eat he stands by to meet whatever other needs they might have.

The visitors engage Abraham in conversation. He soon realizes he is hosting no ordinary visitors, for they know about Sarah's condition and the promise of descendants. When they reaffirm God's promise to produce a child through her, Sarah breaks into laughter. Earlier Abraham had laughed at such a possibility (17:17); now Sarah laughs with incredulity. The image of a pregnant Sarah strains the imagination. Are an old man and woman, well beyond their childbearing years, now to have that long-denied child? Remembering the importance of names in Genesis 17, we now hear that this "soon to be" child of Sarah's will receive the name "Isaac"—*laughter.*

Two of the visitors depart for Sodom; the third delays to talk further with Abraham. God, the third visitor, determines that he will reveal to Abraham his plan to destroy the cities of the plain, cities rampant with a level of injustice that rivals the days of Noah. Both God and his promise bearer Abraham are fully committed to the covenant relationship. God has called Abraham to live in his presence and give himself wholeheartedly to the relationship. Abraham responds faithfully. In a poignant scene, Abraham questions God about *his* justice and righteousness! With considerable courage, Abraham lives up to the confidence God has placed in him. The language is striking.

> The LORD said, "Shall I hide from Abraham what I am about to do, seeing that Abraham shall become a great and mighty nation, and all the nations of the earth shall be blessed in him? No, for I have chosen him, that he may charge his children and his household after him to **keep the way of the LORD by doing righteousness and justice**; so that the LORD may bring about for Abraham what he has promised him." Then the LORD said, "How great is the outcry against Sodom and Gomorrah and how very grave their sin! **I must go down and see** whether they have done altogether according to the outcry that has come to me; and if not, I will know. . . ." Then Abraham came near and said, "Will you indeed sweep away the righteous with the wicked? . . . Far be it from you to do such a thing, to slay the righteous with the wicked, so that the **righteous fare as the wicked**! Far be that from you! Shall not the **Judge of all the earth do what is just**?" (18:17-21,23,25, emphasis added).

The language echoes previous scenes. The Lord *goes down to see* the behavior of the people of Sodom and Gomorrah, just as he earlier had gone down to see the activity at Babel. God reveals his plan to Abraham so that Abraham and his descendants will live before the Lord in righteousness and justice; Abraham in turn questions God concerning the rightness and justice of his plan to destroy these wicked cities. The exchange is noteworthy. Abraham questions the justice of indiscriminately destroying the righteous with the wicked. When Abraham is unable to produce ten righteous inhabitants, the conversation closes. The only matter left is to extract Lot and his family from the area prior to the destruction.

Genesis 19 stands in striking contrast to the preceding chapter, though the scene opens similarly. The two visitors who departed from Abraham's tent arrive at dusk at Sodom. They intend to stay in the city square, but Lot enjoins them to stay at his house. Like Abraham, he is deferential and offers them a meal (though no extravagance is highlighted). That evening, chaos breaks out. If we doubted Abraham's ability to find ten righteous men, we doubt no more. The text informs us that "the men of Sodom, both young and old, *to the last man,* surrounded the [i.e., Lot's] house." They intend sexual abuse of the visitors. Lot goes outside to defuse the situation. His "solution" simultaneously astonishes and appalls us—he offers his daughters as surrogate sex objects in lieu of the visitors! The response of the men of Sodom is dramatic—*"This fellow came here as an alien, and he would play the judge! Now we will deal worse with you than with them."* The men of Sodom are beyond moral reach—they scoff at Lot's attempt to adjudicate the situation and make it abundantly clear he is *not* part of their community.

The tables are turned. Lot, who went out to protect the visitors, now is himself endangered. Lot had earlier *pressed* (*yiptzar*) the visitors to lodge with him; the townsmen now *press* (*yiptzeru*) against Lot to break into the house. However, before the men of Sodom can harm him, the visitors retrieve Lot and strike the city dwellers with blindness, thus rendering ineffectual their plan. The visitors now reveal to Lot the divine plan to destroy the cities of the plain. They instruct Lot to gather his family, including future sons-in-law, and depart. Whereas Abraham attempted to keep Sodom and Gomorrah from destruction, Lot tries to keep from leaving. Lot is irresolute. The scene is tragic. Lot's future sons-in-law do not take him seriously. Though in imminent danger, he leaves reluctantly, and then negotiates a less rigorous exit. Though his life is in serious danger, he requests a shorter journey to a nearby village. When the divine visitors agree, Lot, his wife, and his daughters depart. Though not stated explicitly, Abraham has rescued Lot a second time!

The escape heightens the tragedy. Lot's wife does not survive the departure. Lot, left alone with his daughters, finally decides to move beyond the small village and seek the safety of the rugged hill country. Looking at the devastation wrought across the expanse of the plain, the daughters of Lot determine that they alone are left upon the earth! They intoxicate their father and lay with him so that they may have children and not be left helpless. Earlier Noah, a father who delivered his sons through his own righteousness, experienced the debilitating effects of drunkenness and was shamed by his talkative son. Here Lot, a pathetic father who had earlier been willing to barter his daughters for sexual favors, now unwittingly engages in incest. The moral depravity of a life lived in the shadow of the wickedness of Sodom comes full circle.

Abimelech, Isaac, and Ishmael (Genesis 20–21)

Lot and his family behind us, Genesis 20–21 returns us to the world of Genesis 12 and 16. In Genesis 20 we find Abraham again dealing with a foreign king. This time the king is named—Abimelech of Gerar (Philistia). Genesis 21 takes us back to the earlier struggle between Sarah and Hagar.

Abraham apparently did not learn well in Egypt (or perhaps he learned only too well!). Finding himself apart from the land of promise, he again identifies Sarah as his sister rather than his wife. In contrast to Genesis 12, where he scripted Sarah's speech, here Abraham provides the duplicitous information himself. Like Genesis 12, his actions bring a foreign king and country to the brink of disaster. Abimelech takes Sarah into his harem, but before the relationship can be consummated, God intervenes. Abimelech rightly claims ignorance and innocence of the true nature of Abraham and Sarah's relationship.

Though similar in many details, the differences between Genesis 12 and 20 are what most interest us. In Genesis 20, God engages directly in the conversation. Furthermore, he declares Abraham a prophet. A prophet in the Old Testament is first and foremost a spokesperson for God. Here Abraham is called to intercede for *innocent* Abimelech. The text is a vivid reminder that prophets are not superhuman; their faith may wax and wane like any other believer. Perhaps most strikingly, Abimelech chides Abraham for his behavior—*"What were you thinking of, that you did this thing?"* Abraham can only respond with a feeble assertion that Sarah *technically* is his sister (though this is not her primary relationship to Abraham) and claim his fear that there was *no fear of God* in this place! King Abimelech ironically demonstrates more *fear of God* than Abraham. He does exactly as instructed by God. Again a foreign king enriches Abraham. This time he is not escorted from the land; Abimelech, like Abraham did for Lot, allows Abraham to select whatever portion of land he desires for a possession! The scene closes with Abraham interceding for Abimelech and the land of Gerar returning to its former productivity. Though the language of blessing and curse is not used, the motif is implicit.

Genesis 21 recounts the scene for which we have been impatiently waiting. Pregnant Sarah gives birth to Isaac, the son of Abraham's old age. Laughter rings throughout; joyous laughter supplants the earlier laughter of doubt. No sooner do we wonder whether Abraham is distancing himself from the promise (Genesis 20) than we see him circumcising his son Isaac on the eighth day. The promise is embraced. If Genesis 20 (Abraham and Abimelech) reminds us of Genesis 12 (Abraham and Pharaoh), Genesis 21 returns us to Genesis 16—the first conflict between Sarah and Hagar.

Abraham marks the weaning of Isaac with a lavish festival. However, apparently during the celebration, Sarah sees Ishmael playing. (The Greek translation adds "with her son Isaac.") Though the exact nature of Ishmael's activity is unclear, the wordplay is noteworthy—Sarah saw the son of Hagar *"Isaac-ing"* (*metsacheq*, from the root *tsachaq*—to laugh). Sarah returns to Abraham and demands Hagar and her son be expelled. This time Abraham expedites Hagar's departure. Hagar (and her son Ishmael) will continue to receive God's blessing through Abraham; however, they will not bear God's promise.

Hagar and Ishmael depart into the unforgiving desert. Soon waterless, they seek any shade available. As Hagar begins weeping at their imminent demise, God again *appears* (for Hagar he is *El-Roi*—"God of my seeing") and comforts her. Earlier God told Abraham to *hear the voice* of his wife Sarah (v. 12); now God has *heard* Ishmael's voice (v. 17). This will not be the end of Hagar's story. The God of seeing opens her eyes—there before her is a well of water!

The scene closes where it began—with Abraham and Abimelech. King Abimelech recognizes the presence of God's blessing in the life of Abraham. He calls Abraham to enter into a covenant with him. He asks that Abraham treat him and his descendants with the same loyalty and deference that he has shown Abraham. The covenant language is striking. It will reappear much later in a similar conversation with a foreigner and Israelite spies. At Jericho, Rahab the prostitute enjoins the spies she has hidden and protected to show her the same covenant loyalty and treatment she has shown them (Joshua 2:9-12).

Though Abraham and Abimelech may live under a mutual covenant arrangement, their shepherds compete for limited water resources. Abraham and Abimelech seal their treaty with an exchange of animals (seven lambs) and clear rights to a water well. They both take an oath. The place receives the name Beer-sheba ("well of oath/well of seven"). This time Abraham, in lieu of erecting an altar, plants a tamarisk tree and worships God. Having already acknowledged God as the "Most High" (*El Elyon*) and the "Almighty" (*El Shaddai*), he now worships him as the "Everlasting One" (*El Olam*).

The Akedah—The Binding of Isaac (Genesis 22)

The Abraham cycle reaches a crescendo in chapter 22. The scene, eloquent in its lack of direct discourse, fairly throbs with drama. Abraham's promising God now calls the recipient of his blessings to sacrifice the son of his old age. In Genesis 22 we encounter the watershed moment in the life of Abraham. In the Pentateuch only here does God test an individual; later he will *test* Israel in the wilderness. Literarily, Genesis 22 wraps neatly with the opening scene of Genesis 12. Abraham's life is returning to where it began!

The linkage between Genesis 12 and 22 appears primarily through close literary structuring. Genesis 12 and 22 provide the scenes for the first and last time God will speak with Abraham. In Genesis 12, God called Abraham to "go forth . . . to the land I will show you." In Genesis 22, God calls Abraham to "go forth . . . to the land of Moriah." In Genesis 12, God called Abraham to leave "your land, your homeland, your father's house." In Genesis 22, he calls Abraham to take "your son, your only son, the one whom you love." At Haran Abraham left his father forever; at Moriah Abraham will lose his son forever. At Haran, future reward was promised; at Moriah, no reward is promised, only tremendous loss.

The drama is heightened (if possible) coming immediately on the heels of the expulsion of Hagar and Ishmael from Abraham's house. Earlier Abraham had *placed* bread and water on Hagar's back and sent his firstborn into the desert (21:14); now he *places* the wood on Isaac's back (22:6) and departs for the mountain.

The dialogue is sparse, but incredibly poignant. Isaac consistently calls Abraham *father*; Abraham repeatedly responds with *my son*. To Isaac's query about the lack of a sacrificial animal, Abraham simply replies, *"The Lord will provide."*

The following scene reaches an unbelievable intensity. No words fill the air, for there is nothing to be said. The look between Abraham and his son Isaac has captured the imagination of countless writers and artists throughout the centuries. Altar building is nothing new to Abraham; he has been building altars throughout the land for his God. However, this altar is different, for this altar will seemingly host not the affirmation of the promise, but its recall! As Abraham prepares to slay his son, the Lord intervenes. Words now fill the air:

> But the angel of the LORD called to him from heaven, and said, "Abraham, Abraham!" And he said, "Here I am." He said, "Do not lay your hand on the boy or do anything to him; for now I know that you fear God, since you have not withheld **your son, your only son, from me**" (22:11-12, emphasis added).

Just as Hagar raised her eyes and saw the well the Lord provided, so now Abraham raises his eyes and sees a ram provided for the sacrifice. Abraham fittingly names the place, *Yahweh-yireh*—usually translated "the Lord will provide." However, the phrase plays on the word for "sight" (*ra'ah*), for the Lord has *seen to the offering.* The promise to Abraham is recited a final time:

> The angel of the LORD called to Abraham a second time from heaven, and said, "By myself I have sworn, says the LORD: Because you have done this, and have not withheld your son, your only son, I will indeed bless you, and make your offspring as numerous as the stars of heaven and as the sand that is on the seashore. And your offspring shall possess the gate of their ene-

mies, and by your offspring shall all the nations gain blessing for themselves, because you have obeyed my voice" (22:15-18).

The Epilogue (Genesis 23–25)

The pinnacle of the Abraham cycle has been reached. Only closure is lacking. The final chapters of the Abraham cycle prepare us for the transfer of the blessing to the next generation. Abraham has two crucial transactions to execute. At one end of the spectrum, he must secure a burial place for Sarah (chapter 23). At the other end of the spectrum, he must secure a wife for Isaac (chapter 24).

Genesis 23 recounts Abraham's securing of an appropriate burial location for the ancestress of the promise. The scene is replete with ancient Near Eastern negotiating niceties and property law. The final paragraph reads almost like a legal contract. In a fascinating dialogue, Abraham presents himself as a "stranger and alien" to the Hittites residing in the area. The Hittites negate his self-effacement, designating him a *"mighty prince."* Our minds return to that earlier scene with Lot and the men of Sodom. In Genesis 19, the men of Sodom refused Lot's attempt to "judge" a situation, labeling him an "alien" in their region. Our final image of Lot is that of a manipulated father, homeless in a cave. In contrast, Abraham, a savvy negotiator, secures a burial cave with attendant field in the heartland of Canaan.

Abraham will not bargain for this piece of property. The God with whom he has entered into covenant has enriched him; he needs no financial assistance from earthly agents. He pays what may be an exorbitant price; Sarah will rest in dignity. In death they possess the land; they are no longer merely sojourning strangers.

Having secured a burial place, Abraham turns his attention to securing Isaac's future. The account provides rich detail, from Abraham's instructions to his servant Eliezer to Eliezer's execution of those instructions. Abraham will neither allow Isaac to leave the land of promise nor allow him to marry a native of that land. A return to Haran is a must. A bride must be secured, but a bride willing to abandon family and journey to the promised land. She will share in Abraham's story and journey. We will treat the marriage of Isaac in detail in the next chapter. At this stage, suffice it to say that Isaac functions primarily as a hinge between Abraham and his grandson Jacob. He is a transitional figure, providing a bridge from Abraham to Jacob.

The Abraham cycle concludes with the subsequent marriage of Abraham to Keturah. Although she provides him numerous children, it is made clear that no one will supplant Isaac as bearer of the promise. Like Ishmael, these children are blessed, but not called. Abraham dies at 175. The segments of his life are easily remembered—75 years in Ur and Haran, 25 years waiting for Isaac, 75 years in Canaan after Isaac's birth.

Finding Ourselves in Genesis 16–23

The Abraham cycle provides us rich theological and spiritual resources. As mentioned in the last chapter, Abraham's story is *our* story. This is not simply some archaic history lesson or walk down memory lane; rather, it is the story of our ancestor in the faith, whose life of faith mirrors our life of faith.

Although Abraham can be viewed from multiple angles, the interplay of faith and fear offers a profitable vantage point from which to view his life. When Abraham fully embraces the call of God with its promises, he manifests faith. When he distances himself from that call and promise, he demonstrates fear. In Abraham we take courage, for we realize that life is never as simple as a single declaration of faith, never to need re-visiting. Abraham's life is a journey, and journeys frequently take unexpected turns, seemingly endless delays, and hazards. As Abraham journeys through the land, he repeatedly constructs altars, claiming the location for his promising God. In response to God's total commitment to the relationship in Genesis 15, Abraham fully commits with the sign of circumcision in Genesis 17. At times Abraham demonstrates tremendous faith in spite of events that are baffling, ambiguous, and contradictory. Abraham reminds us through the nature of his life that faith is more than mere assent to a proposition or an intellectual exercise. Faith manifests itself in active obedience and demonstrated trust. The life of Abraham also reminds us that God's promises do not always come to realization overnight. Abraham experiences pilgrimage 25 years waiting for the promised heir to arrive! Like Abraham, we live between the "already" and the "not yet." We have fully experienced the initial installment of the promises of God, but the complete realization of those promises awaits us. In that interim, we live as *pilgrims*.

■ Contrast personal examples of embracing God's call and distancing yourself from it.
■ Give some examples from your own life when God's promises were delayed. Looking back, have you accepted God's timing?

In a society given to instant gratification and enamored with immediate results, the life of Abraham reminds us that a crucial element of faith is patient waiting upon the Lord. This in no way intimates that we sit by quietly; Abraham repeatedly engages his Lord. He questions the justice of action taken against Sodom. When no righteous persons surface, Abraham quietly departs, having received his answer.

Perhaps more importantly, the life of Abraham reminds us of the true purpose of blessing. We live in a world obsessed with receiving blessings from God. Abraham the blessed shows us the true meaning of blessing. Being blessed by God has *functional* reality. In his most faithful moments, Abraham refuses to hoard the blessings God has bestowed upon him, realizing God gave them to be disbursed. Though we often shamelessly hoard the divine blessings, Abraham calls us to remember the true purpose of our calling. God declares through Abraham that he wills to bless his creatures.

Life is not always simple; the path is not always straight and well lit. Abraham reminds us of the nature of life when we doubt God's ability to fulfill his promises and provide protection. Ironically, Abraham's most tenuous moments are those when he attempts to "help" God or to fulfill the divine promises through his own devices! Consistently conflict supplants blessing and peace. We take comfort, realizing that God's choice of Abraham says more about God than Abraham. This is the scandal of the gospel. God chooses Abraham, *and us*, not because of who *we are*, but because of *who he is*. Repeatedly God eschews the obvious candidates for calling and instead bestows his blessings upon those seemingly least likely to effect change. God's heroes are the unlikeliest of candidates—Moses, Hannah, Ruth, David, Zechariah and Elizabeth, Mary and Joseph. The list goes on. Paul helpfully reminds us we are a part of that lineage:

Consider your own call, brothers and sisters: not many of you were wise by human standards, not many were powerful, not many were of noble birth. But God chose what is foolish in the world to shame the wise; God chose what is weak in the world to shame the strong; God chose what is low and despised in the world, things that are not, to reduce to nothing things that are, so that no one might boast in the presence of the God. He is the source of your life in Christ Jesus, who became for us wisdom from God, and righteousness and sanctification and redemption" (1 Corinthians 1:26-30).

Paul reminds us that we, like Abraham, cannot be righteous by ourselves. Only in relationship with God do we become righteous.

We see this most dramatically reflected in the life of Abraham, when "righteous Gentiles" call Abraham to account. No moment would have been more striking to an ancient Israelite audience than the exchange between King Abimelech and Abraham. Who could imagine—a foreign king delivering a lesson in ethics to the premier father of God's people? Repeatedly Abraham realigns himself with God's ways and wills. Just as Abraham learns a wonderful lesson about covenant from Abimelech, so the spies at Jericho later learn about covenant loyalty from the Canaanite prostitute Rahab (Joshua 2:9-12). The Old and New Testaments are checkered with examples of "outsiders" teaching God's people. Such is perhaps the backdrop for Jesus' statement in Matthew 8:11:

"Truly I tell you, in no one in Israel [in reference to the centurion at Capernaum] have I found such faith. I tell you, many will come from east and west and will eat with Abraham and Isaac and Jacob in the kingdom of heaven. . . ."

■ What are some examples of hoarding God's blessings?
■ Who are some unlikely heroes of faith that you have known?

In striking contrast stands Lot. Lot stands so close to Abraham genetically, and yet so far spiritually. Lot sadly shows us the nature of life when the promises of God are discounted, if not denied. Lot is ridiculed by those nearest him geographically (the inhabitants of Sodom), he is not taken seriously by those about to enter his own house (his future sons-in-law), he finishes his life powerless with his future charted by his desperate daughters.

Finally, Abraham reminds us that embracing the promise is seldom easy or without cost. Genesis 22 is the radical epitome of the cost of pilgrimage with God. Genesis 22, known in Judaism as the Akedah ("Binding") of Isaac, is possibly the most preached and discussed text among rabbis. The text fairly bristles with drama and difficulties. Not surprisingly, commentators often focus more on what is left unsaid (e.g., what did Sarah think of all this? What was the relationship between Abraham and Isaac after this incident?) than on what the text says.

The place of Genesis 22 in the larger Abraham cycle is strategic. At one level, Genesis 22 forces us to return once more to Genesis 12:1-3. In the light of God's promise of land and descendants, calling upon Abraham to sacrifice the long-awaited descendant seems illogical, if not absurd. Just as Genesis 12 opens with a call to Abraham to journey forth to receive a promised land and descendants, so Genesis 22 calls Abraham to journey forth with the embodiment of that promise and relinquish it. More specifically, asking Abraham to rid himself of a(nother) son, after just losing Ishmael (Genesis 21:8-21), seemingly borders on cruelty.

Two themes dominate Genesis 22—divine testing and divine providing. The testing of Abraham is poignant—having committed himself fully to the covenant promises (Genesis 15), God now tests Abraham to discover if he is fully committed to those same promises. Amazingly, rather than articulate his concerns about the divine testing, Abraham repeatedly affirms his conviction regarding divine provision. Throughout the narrative Abraham never wavers from his conviction that God will provide. Significantly, we are never told what Abraham understands that provision to entail. Abraham's language is important. Genesis 22 wants us to know that Abraham's obedience is not "blind obedience"; rather, it is rooted in his trust in God's fidelity to his promises.

Within the larger context of these twin themes of divine testing and providence, several noteworthy sub-themes surface. The poignancy of the moment is captured three times by the description of Isaac—*"your son, **your only** son"* (vv. 2,12,16). Three times Abraham responds with "here I am" (vv. 1,11 [to God], 7 [to Isaac—expanded to *"here I am, **my son**"*]). Abraham has repeatedly built altars to publicize his commitment to the divine call; now he is called to construct the ultimate altar. Throughout the narrative, sight plays a central role. Abraham's sight is mentioned in vv. 4,13; God's sight is acknowledged in his providing (vv. 8, 14 [twice]). "Abraham places his trust in *God's seeing.*"

- On the one hand, Genesis 22 beckons us to ask, "What is at stake in this for God?"
- On the other hand, Genesis 22 compels us to ask, "What is at stake in this for Abraham (and for us)?"

This text counters a most fundamental human instinct. Not surprisingly, "survival" shows vie for popularity on our TV screens and in our theaters. Years ago the noted Holocaust writer E. Wiesel published a sermon on Genesis 22 entitled, "Isaac, a Survivor's Story." Our drive to survive couples nicely with a most popular contemporary view of God—God as giver. Our religious world is saturated with the theology that God not only wants us to survive, but also wants us to have an abundant life (most commonly characterized as abundance of possessions). Against this backdrop, Genesis 22 rightly makes us uncomfortable, if not terrified!

If we can get beyond the shock of God asking a father to take the life of his only son, we realize even more is at stake for Abraham. In reality, Isaac is more than a son, he is the *embodiment* of the promise finally actualized. Although tenuous at times, the land portion of the promise to Abraham has been largely realized. In contrast, the promise of an heir has been painfully slow in coming. Now, God is inexplicably recalling that portion of the promise. In a very real sense, Abraham, a man previously cut off from his past (Mesopotamia), now hears God recalling his future! If we are not careful, we will tend to abstract this text and sink to moralization (e.g., "the great thing was that Abraham loved God so much he was willing to give him the *best*"!).

In reality, Genesis 22 epitomizes Abraham's entire life! The text acknowledges Abraham's life as journey, his life as test (will he embrace or distance himself from the call?), and his life as trust in the promises of God.

- Give personal examples of when your faith was not only tested but also when God provided.

In the New Testament, Jesus articulates a similarly "terrifying" call. The haunting call of Jesus finds clearest expression in Mark 8:34-35:

> "If any want to become my followers, let them deny themselves and take up their cross and follow me. For those who want to save their life will lose it, and those who lose their life for my sake, and for the sake of the gospel, will save it."

The disciples considered the notion of a crucified Messiah scandalous; surely there was no future in that! Even more importantly, to define discipleship as sacrifice and loss of life remains the greatest challenge for contemporary followers of Christ. Perhaps here is where we ultimately link our story with that of Abraham. Just as Abraham's obedience was not "blind," but rooted firmly in his recognition and affirmation of a God who had fully committed himself to Abraham in word and deed (Genesis 15), so the call of Jesus Christ to sacrifice our future is rooted firmly, not in blind obedience, but in our vision of the crucified and resurrected Lord.

> *Like the God of Abraham, God does not call us to do something he himself is unwilling to do.*

Time has a tendency to diminish weaknesses and enhance abilities. Distance often makes our ancestral heroes "larger than life." At times this impacts us as we approach Scripture. We assume we cannot relate to the ancient biblical characters, since they were heroic in their faith and consistently succeeded where we often experience failure. A close reading of Genesis disabuses us of such fears. Our ancestors in the faith manifest weaknesses and failure of nerve like us. Their stories are our stories.

CHAPTER 7

"Will the Older Serve the Younger?"

(Genesis 24–28)

ith Jacob we enter a new world, yet without leaving the old world behind. Whereas Abraham is consistently called the father of a multitude, Jacob is never defined by fatherhood (even though he has a multitude of descendants). Rather, Jacob both is Israel and *becomes* Israel! In their ancestor Jacob the people of Israel saw their own history writ large. The portrayal of Jacob is remarkably lifelike and realistic. No effort is made to glaze over Jacob's numerous shortcomings and failures. While Jacob certainly does not endear himself to us, neither are we able to walk away from him. Perhaps the most amazing aspect of the Jacob narrative is that God realizes his promises through this character.

The larger structure of the Jacob cycle is worthy of note. Genealogies of the *outsiders* bracket the narrative. The opening scene of the narrative, the birth of Jacob and Esau, is immediately preceded by the genealogy of Ishmael (25:12-18), the son not chosen. Immediately following the final scene of the Jacob narrative is an extensive genealogy of Esau (36:1-43), another son not chosen. The Jacob cycle revolves around four key appearances of God: the divine message to Rebekah regarding the twins wrestling in her uterus (25:23); the first divine appearance to Jacob at Bethel (28:10-22); the realization of the presence of God in the wrestling match at the Jabbok River (32:22-32); the final divine appearance to Jacob at Bethel (35:9-15). The narrative is structured in such a manner that we repeatedly find ourselves returning to earlier portions of the story and rereading them with a heightened understanding and awareness of the impact earlier events will have upon later events. The outline (Outline 4) on page 116 captures some of the interplay in the narrative.

It will surprise some that I begin this chapter on the Jacob narratives with Isaac rather than Jacob. We all know people who have the (mis)fortune of being known primarily by their relationship to someone else. Such is the case with Isaac. In the patriarchal narratives, Isaac is best known as the son of Abraham and father of

OUTLINE 4 ■

(A) Prologue (25:19-24)

  (B) Isaac and the Canaanites: Conflict and Covenant (26)

   (C) JACOB AND ESAU: DECEPTION (27)

    (D) Bethel: Departure (28:10-22)

      (E) Jacob and Laban: Deception and Reconciliation (29–31)

     (D) Mahanaim: Return (32:1-2)

    (C) JACOB AND ESAU: RECONCILIATION (32–33)

  (B) Jacob and the Canaanites: Deception and Enmity (34)

(A) The Edomites (36)

Jacob. He functions as a bridge to transfer the blessing of Abraham to Jacob. The lines between the Abraham narratives and the Jacob narratives are somewhat fuzzy. Information about Isaac appears at the conclusion of the Abraham narrative and at the beginning of the Jacob cycle. I have chosen to discuss Isaac in this chapter simply for convenience sake.

Similarly, the break between the two chapters in this book on Jacob (chapters 7 and 8) is somewhat arbitrary. Jacob's life stands between two great bookends—his departure from the land of promise (Genesis 28), and his re-entry into the land of promise (Genesis 32). At both points in his life he will experience a dramatic encounter with the Lord. Accordingly, I have chosen to treat in chapter 7 the activities that led to his departure from the land of Canaan. In chapter 8 I will treat his activities outside the land of promise and his eventual return.

Isaac and Rebekah (Genesis 24)

Genesis 22 recounts the remarkable call of Abraham to sacrifice his son Isaac, the son who embodies the long-awaited realization of the promise in Genesis 12. Abraham moves faithfully forward to fulfill these mind-boggling divine instructions. This supreme test of Abraham's faith demonstrates his conviction that *"the Lord will provide."* Isaac survives this test of faith and will carry the promise forward. Genesis 24 recounts a pivotal event in the realization of the promise God made to Abraham that he would have descendants too numerous to count. Genesis 24 relates the securing of a wife for Isaac, the child of promise.

The story is delightfully recounted in its entirety. The larger narrative unfolds in eight scenes: Abraham commissions his senior servant Eliezer to find a wife for his son Isaac (vv. 1-9); the servant requests a sign from the Lord (vv. 10-14); Rebekah fulfills the sign (vv. 15-20); she further states that she is Abraham's kin (vv. 21-27); Eliezer is welcomed into her household (vv. 28-33); Eliezer recounts to Rebekah's family his sign and asks them to send Rebekah for marriage to his master (vv. 34-49); Rebekah's family sends her away with a blessing (vv. 50-61); Rebekah and Isaac are married (vv. 62-67).

The story is told simply and progresses easily. In contrast to later scenes that will tax the interpretive skills of the reader, this narrative is a model of clarity. The chapter reflects the masterful touch of the narrator. In good narrative fashion, seemingly "innocent" details are mentioned that allow the reader to return repeatedly to the story and make connections with earlier and later narratives.

In the opening scene, Abraham makes clear to his senior servant Eliezer that this son of promise, unlike his brother Ishmael, will not marry a local Canaanite. Equally importantly, he will not send his son away from the land of promise to secure a wife! He entrusts this most important task to Eliezer (whom we met earlier in Genesis 15), "who had charge of all that he (i.e., Abraham) had." Abraham enters into a covenant agreement with Eliezer, and seals it with an oath and ritual:

> *"Put your hand under my thigh and I will make you swear by the LORD, the God of heaven and earth that you will not get a wife for my son from the daughters of the Canaanites, among whom I live, but will go to my country and to my kindred and get a wife for my son Isaac"* (24:2-3).

Though the ceremony may seem strange to us, Eliezer clearly recognizes the gravity of the oath he is taking. Placing his hand under Abraham's thigh (near his reproductive organ?) signifies that he is handling the procreative essence of the promise God made to Abraham. Eliezer appropriately inquires about the risks involved. He may be unable to find a woman willing to leave home and family and journey forth into an unfamiliar land. Abraham absolves Eliezer of blame should this occur.

Eliezer gathers ten camels and sets forth for the old country. At evening he comes upon a well near a city. He prays, *"O LORD, God of my master Abraham, please grant me success today and show steadfast love to my master Abraham"* (24:12). He devises a sign (though this term is not used) by which he will determine God's answer to his prayer. In the ancient Near East (as to this day) the young women were often entrusted with the task of watering the family livestock. Given the culture, we are not surprised that numerous significant events occur at wells. (Jacob will later meet Rachel at a well; Moses will meet Zipporah at a well.)

A young woman named Rebekah, whom we will soon learn is kin to Abraham, with no prompting or coaching, performs the tasks Eliezer designated for determining the person God had selected. The scene is poignant and narrated succinctly—*"The man [Eliezer] gazed at her [Rebekah] in silence to learn whether or not the LORD had made his journey successful"* (24:21). Having received an affirmative response, Eliezer bestows gifts upon Rebekah and requests lodging for the night. Like her kin Abraham, she is a model of ancient Near Eastern hospitality. She quickly offers room and lodging for Eliezer and his attendants, as well as food for his camels.

When they arrive at her dwelling, we meet Laban (Rebekah's brother) for the first time. He is taken with the gifts this stranger has given his sister. If we know the sequel to this story, we are not surprised that the text chooses to tell us about Laban's reaction to the gifts (v. 30) and to the news that his kin Abraham is incredibly wealthy (vv. 34-36). Eliezer recounts in detail the instructions he received from his master and the sequence of events that have brought him to this point in time. Rebekah's brother Laban (and father Bethuel) quickly agree to give her in marriage to Isaac. With the betrothal secured, lavish gifts are given Laban and Rebekah's mother.

The following morning, Eliezer readies his return to the land of promise and the completion of his vow to his master. However, Laban and his mother attempt to delay the departure. When Eliezer objects, they call Rebekah and allow her to make the decision about the timing of her leaving. She willingly agrees to go immediately. The scene closes with Rebekah receiving a blessing from her family (v. 60) and her marriage to Isaac.

Two notes merit comment. First, careful readers will recognize in the call of Rebekah to leave her family and land language similar to the call of Abraham in Genesis 12. The text makes sure we understand that Rebekah is an essential link in moving the divine promise forward. Genesis 24 echoes key themes of Genesis 12:1-3. Second, Isaac first meets Rebekah in the Negeb (the southern desert region of Israel) after having departed from Beer-lehai-roi (the site where Hagar learned she would give birth to Ishmael). Genesis 24 stands in contrast to Genesis 21. As Hagar moves away from Abraham and the promise, Rebekah now moves toward the promise bearer and becomes a member of the Abrahamic household. She will soon give birth to another promise bearer.

The Birth of Jacob and Esau—Round #1 (Genesis 25)

The opening scene provides a pre-emptive overview of all the major themes that will occur in the Jacob narrative. Rebekah, like Sarah her mother-in-law, initially experiences barrenness. Isaac prays for Rebekah and she becomes pregnant. (Although the response seems immediate, about 20 years elapse.) Genesis 3 has prepared us to expect difficult pregnancies and painful deliveries, and Rebekah fulfills that expectation dramatically. She is pregnant with twins, twins seemingly determined to engage in battle! Conflict will swirl about Jacob throughout his life, with much of the conflict his own doing.

In response to Rebekah's despairing cry for relief, the text quickly informs us that this birth and the story of the lives of these two brothers is no private matter. The histories of two nations are at stake:

And the LORD said to her, "Two nations are in your womb, and two peoples born of you shall be divided; the one shall be stronger than the other, the elder shall serve the younger" (25:23).

The birth of the twins is unforgettable. Wordplays dominate the scene. The first son exits with his heel in the grip of his younger brother. Having been told that the birth of these twin sons anticipates the "birth" of two nations, the text next uses wordplays to highlight that pronouncement. Esau receives his name because he is "ruddy" (*'admoni*, a play on Edom, the designation for Esau's descendants) and "hairy" (*se`ar*, perhaps a play on Seir, the region where Esau will eventually settle). Later Esau the "red man" will demand that Jacob his brother give him some of the "red stuff" (*'adom*) he has just cooked. Since the second brother held Esau's heel in his grip, they name him Jacob (*ya`aqob*)—"heel grabber" (*`aqeb*). The two sons are as different as night and day. Esau is an outdoorsman; he hunts and spends time in the field. Jacob is an "indoorsman"; he lives quietly in the tents (most likely a reference to the life of a herdsman—note the source of meat for the meal Jacob later serves his father). Isaac showers his attention upon Esau; Rebekah prefers Jacob.

The first episode following the birth of the two sons captures the character of each. Esau, the firstborn and favorite of his father, carries the birthright (*bekorah*) and potential paternal blessing (*berakah*). Having just returned from an unsuccessful hunting trip, Esau enters the kitchen. Famished, he demands that Jacob give him some of the stew he is cooking. Esau clearly lives at the gut level. Jacob, realizing his brother's impetuous and compulsive nature, strikes an incredible bargain. He exchanges a meal for his older brother's birthright! Esau exchanges a long-term benefit for an immediate gain. The text graphically summarizes Esau's cavalier treatment of his most prized possession—"*he despised his birthright*" (a term used elsewhere of the attitude of Eli's sons to the Lord [1 Samuel 2:30] and David's treatment of Uriah [2 Samuel 12:9]).

Esau's disregard for his status as firstborn is more than matched by Jacob's desire for such a position. In Jacob we encounter a sharp mind with little conscience. Jacob is appropriately named, for in Hebrew the idiom for deceiver or trickster is "heel-grabber." Jacob will spend his life scheming to supplant his brother and dealing with the consequences of his often less than honorable deceptions. With Jacob we have moved from the "faithful Abraham" through the "successful Isaac" to the "scheming Jacob."

Isaac and Abimelech (Genesis 26)

Genesis 26 takes us back to earlier events in the life of Abraham in Genesis 12 and 20. In those earlier encounters with foreign kings, Abraham instructed Sarah to identify him as her brother rather than husband. In both instances difficulties arose. Genesis 26 contains the only detailed narrative in which Isaac stands on center stage. Famine breaks out in the land, making water an even more precious commodity. However, God instructs Isaac not to migrate to Egypt, but to "settle in the land that I will show you" (echoes of Genesis 12:1). Just as Abraham refused to let Isaac depart the land of promise to secure a wife, so now God instructs Isaac not to leave that land for Egypt. Instead, God sends Isaac to the Philistine territory of King Abimelech, whom we met in Genesis 20.

The chapter falls out into five sections: Isaac's journey to Gerar; Rebekah's adventure in Gerar; Isaac's prosperity and departure from Abimelech's region; repeated disputes over wells; a peace treaty made at Beersheba. The narrative allows us to look backward and forward at the same time. As we read the story of the encounter between Isaac and Abimelech, we are reminded of the promises God made to Abraham. The chapter repeatedly affirms that the promises given Abraham are intact in Isaac. In fact, when the promise is articulated, it is somewhat expanded in scope.

> *Reside in this land as an alien, and I will be with you, and will bless you; for to you and to your descendants I will give all these lands, and I will fulfill the oath that I swore to your father Abraham. I will make your offspring as numerous as the stars of heaven, and will give to your offspring **all these lands**; and all the nations of the earth shall gain blessing for themselves through your offspring, because Abraham obeyed my voice and kept my charge, my commandments, my statutes, and my laws* (26:3-5, emphasis added).

The narrative also looks forward. Isaac the son of promise bears the blessings of the Lord. Isaac's wealth and prosperity generate conflict with Abimelech's countrymen.

> *Isaac sowed seed in that land, and in the same year reaped a hundredfold. The LORD blessed him, and the man became rich; he prospered more and more until he became very wealthy. He had possessions of flocks and herds, and a great household, so that the Philistines envied him. (Now the Philistines had stopped up and filled with earth all the wells that his father's servants had dug in the days of his father Abraham.) And Abimelech said to Isaac, "Go away from us; you have become too powerful for us"* (26:12-16).

Against this backdrop, it becomes clear that two incidents trigger a tense encounter between Abimelech and Isaac. One involves Rebekah; the other involves the scarcity of water. The first occurs when Abimelech sees Isaac and Rebekah interacting in such a way that Abimelech realizes their relationship is not that of a brother and sister. The language is intriguing. Though often translated "fondling," the Hebrew actually uses the same root from which Isaac's name derives. That is, King Abimelech saw Isaac *"Isaac-ing"* (*metsacheq*) his wife. (This is the same term used earlier for Ishmael's treatment of Isaac in 21:9.) Like his father Abraham, Isaac receives a stern lecture from a foreign king. Although Isaac has just received divine confirmation of his father's promise, he acts out of fear. The second episode, the struggle over water rights and envy of the Philistines over Isaac's success, causes him to pack his bags and depart the region.

Although moving out of the immediate vicinity, Isaac's success seemingly causes the Philistines to follow him and contest each place he settles. Rivalry dominates the landscape. Whether unearthing old wells (dug by Abraham) or digging new wells, the Philistines fight for possession. Isaac digs three wells; the first two he concedes to the Philistines and appropriately names them Esek ("quarrel") and Sitnah ("opposition"). It is only when he digs the third well that he is free from Philistine opposition. He fittingly names it Rehoboth ("wide spaces").

Apparently not content with the distance between himself and the Philistines, Isaac moves again to the region of Beersheba. His first night back in the region, God appears to him and reiterates the promise. The language is noteworthy: *"I am the God of your father Abraham;* ***do not be afraid,*** *for I am with you and will bless you and make your offspring numerous for my servant Abraham's sake"* (26:24). There he not only digs a well, but also like his father before him, builds an altar.

Genesis 26 closes with a fascinating scene. A contingent of Philistine state officials come to Isaac at Beersheba and seek to enter into a non-aggression pact. The tables are turned. Having hassled Isaac, they now acknowledge the blessings they have received from Isaac's presence in their midst. They speak loftily of their honorable treatment of Isaac (a somewhat selective recounting of recent events!) and seek blessing from him rather than harm. With this closing scene, we receive further confirmation that Isaac truly bears the Abrahamic promise and blessing—even foreigners recognize such!

Jacob and Esau—Round #2 (Genesis 27)

Our first encounter with Esau and Jacob has prepared us well for this dramatic moment in the history of Abraham's successors. Isaac is aged and functionally blind. He determines to pass on the blessing to his firstborn Esau. Though somewhat ambiguous, it seems that the bestowal of the blessing officializes the birthright— the rights of the firstborn. Documents from the ancient Near East suggest that such a ceremony typically occurred toward the end of the father's life. By birth order Esau has the *birthright* (*bekorah*); Isaac now desires to acknowledge the benefits (that is, *blessings* [*berakah*]) that go with that birthright. Already having been told that Isaac favors Esau, partly because of his love of the outdoors and hunting, Isaac now commissions Esau to secure wild game so that Isaac may bestow the blessing with appropriate fanfare. Esau, obedient to his father's wishes, departs for the field.

With Esau's absence, Rebekah acts quickly to move her favorite son to the front of the line. Just as Isaac instructed Esau, so Rebekah now instructs Jacob. Jacob should secure goat meat for her to prepare a feast. Since Isaac cannot see, the ruse should work. Jacob's stew secured the *birthright* from his brother; now his mother's stew will secure the *blessing*. However, like Jacob, we remember that Esau is noted *both* for his ruddy complexion and his hairy exterior. Jacob fears the deception, if exposed, will bring him curse, rather than blessing. Rebekah quickly devises a contingency plan. She takes clothing Esau has left with her and dresses Jacob in it. She then takes skins from the recently slaughtered goats and covers those areas Isaac is most prone to touch—his hands and neck.

Isaac is immediately suspicious when Jacob, thinly disguised as Esau, enters. The time lapse for even a successful hunt seems incredibly brief. Since Isaac is functionally blind, his other senses compensate. Isaac must have experienced significant confusion, for he recognizes the voice; it is Jacob's. The "proof of identity" comes with touch. The son before him is hairy. Though still seemingly suspicious (the father repeatedly questions his son concerning his identity), Isaac confirms the (mistaken) identity through smell. When Jacob bends to kiss his father, he recognizes the smell of Esau's garments. (Just as Jacob deceives his father with a garment, so later Jacob's sons will deceive their father with a garment!)

The ruse has worked. Isaac pronounces the blessing upon his son:

*"Ah, the smell of my son is like the smell of a field that the
LORD has blessed. May God give you of the dew of heaven, and
of the fatness of the earth, and plenty of grain and wine. Let peoples serve you, and nations bow down to you. Be lord over your
brothers, and may your mother's sons bow down to you. Cursed
be everyone who curses you, and blessed be everyone who blesses you!"* (27:27-29).

The son who "smells like a field" will enjoy the prosperity of those
fields. However, he has little time to enjoy the moment. Jacob initially feared his fate should his father discover his ruse. However, we
soon realize his concern should be with his brother, not his father.

No sooner is the blessing pronounced than Esau enters with
the sumptuous feast he has prepared in anticipation of the blessing he is to receive. When Esau realizes he is the victim of a terri-
ble deception, he cries out in anguish. Earlier Esau may have been
a gullible fool (about the "red stuff"); now he is an innocent victim.
Angrily he declares:

*"Is he not rightly named Jacob [ya`aqob]? For he has sup-
planted [literally, "out-Jacobed"—waya`qbeni] me these two
times. He took away my birthright; and look, now he has taken
away my blessing"* (27:36).

Esau pleads for a blessing, but Isaac informs him that a pronounced
blessing is like an oath—once spoken, it cannot be reversed. The
movement from Jacob to Esau is complete. Isaac calls Jacob my son
seven times in the course of their conversation; he calls Esau my son
only once! The birthright (and blessing) Esau previously treated so
cavalierly has suddenly become an obsession. Esau presses until
Isaac pronounces a "reverse blessing" upon Esau:

*"See, **away from** the fatness of the earth shall your home be,
and **away from** the dew of heaven on high. By your sword you
shall live, and you shall serve your brother; but when you break
loose, you shall break his yoke from your neck"* (27:39-40,
emphasis added).

Rebekah, having executed her plan to perfection, now moves swiftly to protect her recently blessed son. The blessing that was to bring peace to all peoples now is encircled by conflict. Rebekah earlier boldly announced that she would willingly accept any curse that might come if her plan failed. Now she realizes that the curse might be nothing less than the loss of both her sons (the younger through execution by his brother, the older possibly through execution for murder). (In truth she will never see her favorite son again.) She first prepares Jacob for a journey to the old country, the land of her origins. She then cunningly goes before Isaac and plays upon a source of irritation. In blatant contrast to the family pattern, Esau had married *"women of the land."* Esau's marital decisions had brought Isaac and Rebekah much bitterness (26:34-35). Rebekah now enjoins Isaac to send Jacob to the land of her (and his) ancestors, so that he may secure a proper bride.

Esau makes one final (and futile) attempt to secure his father's blessing. To ameliorate his parents' irritation over his marital choices, Esau marries a daughter of Ishmael. The decision has limited effectiveness—like Ishmael, Esau will share in Abraham's blessing, but not in the promise and covenant.

Jacob's Departure and Dream at Bethel (Genesis 28)

What Abraham had denied to Isaac (to depart the land of promise), Isaac now allows for Jacob. He instructs Jacob to journey to his mother's ancestral land, and there secure a wife. He pronounces another blessing upon his son, a blessing that acknowledges that he is heir to the promise of Abraham:

> *"May God Almighty [El Shaddai] bless you and make you fruitful and numerous, that you may become a company of peoples. May he give to you the blessing of Abraham, to you and to your offspring with you, so that you may take possession of the land where you now live as an alien—land that God gave to Abraham"* (28:3-4).

Jacob's departure to the land of Haran presents us a most intriguing dilemma. For the first time, the actual bearer of the Abrahamic promise is returning to the old country—the land of pre-promise! Simply put, the Abrahamic promise is going in reverse! Earlier the promise bearer has departed the land of promise during tenuous times. Both Abraham and Isaac manifested fear rather than faith in those prior circumstances. In response, the God who called them repeatedly manifested his commitment to the recipients of his blessing. However, this is the first time the promise is in *retreat*. We cannot help but wonder, will the God of the promise go with the promise bearer?

Our answer comes quickly. Jacob, weary from a long day of travel, stops at sundown to spend the night. Using a rock for his pillow, he falls asleep, only to begin dreaming. In his dream he envisions a staircase (possibly on the order of a ziggurat) reaching to heaven. Only angelic beings are ascending and descending the staircase. No human beings ascend this staircase to heaven. Stationed at the top of the staircase is none other than God! He hears God speaking:

> "I am the LORD, the God of Abraham your father and the God of Isaac; the land on which you lie I will give to you and to your offspring; and your offspring shall be like the dust of the earth, and you shall spread abroad to the west and to the east and to the north and to the south; and all the families of the earth shall be blessed in you and in your offspring. Know that I am with you and will keep you wherever you go, and will bring you back to this land; for I will not leave you until I have done what I have promised you" (28:13-15).

The dream startles Jacob; he awakes and reacts like his forefathers Abraham and Isaac—with fear. However, more importantly, he recognizes the momentous nature of this occasion. Jacob realizes the singular nature of this moment and his situation. He stands at a most unusual crossroads. Behind him lies the land of promise *and* his past, a past of anger and alienation. Before him looms his future, a future of uncertainty and anxious hope. Intersecting these two roads from above and descending to meet him is the promise and presence of God! Jacob will not travel alone; the God who called his grandfather Abraham out of Haran will escort Jacob back to Haran! His journey for survival can become a journey of faith.

Jacob fully engages the promise, but engages in a manner typical to his nature. He takes his rocky pillow and stations it as a monumental pillar, consecrating it with oil. He names the place Bethel, for this location is none other than the *house of God (beth-'el)*. True to his character, he makes a vow, but a *conditional* vow.

> *"If God will be with me, and will keep me in this way that I go, and will give me bread to eat and clothing to wear, so that I come again to my father's house in peace, then the* LORD *shall be my God, and this stone, which I have set up for a pillar, shall be God's house; and of all that you give me I will surely give one tenth to you"* (28:20-22).

On a more positive note, Jacob allows the reality of his dream to trump his old world of fear and anxiety. Jacob recognizes and acknowledges the awesomeness of the God of his ancestors. Negatively, his vow is *conditioned* upon God fulfilling his just spoken promise. Jacob has not fully divorced himself from his manipulative ways.

Finding Ourselves in Genesis 24–28

Time has a tendency to diminish weaknesses and enhance abilities. Distance often makes our ancestral heroes "larger than life." At times this impacts us as we approach Scripture. We assume we cannot relate to the ancient biblical characters, since they were heroic in their faith and consistently succeeded where we often experience failure. A close reading of Genesis disabuses us of such fears. Our ancestors in the faith manifest weaknesses and failure of nerve like us. Their stories are *our* stories.

Abraham compels us to rethink the interplay in our lives between fear and faith. His story calls us to reconsider those times when we distance ourselves from the promises of God, or think we must *supplement* God's promises with our own plans. Like Abraham, we experience the problems that result from such decisions. Conversely, as heirs to the promises of Abraham, we also know those joyous occasions when we fully embrace the promises of God and experience the blessings that come from walking faithfully with God. Abraham, our father in the faith, charts the path for us.

When we come to the Jacob cycle the waters become murkier. Under our breaths, we cannot help but ask ourselves, "How could God choose such a rascal to bestow his blessings upon humankind?" Jacob appears as cunning and conniving, repeatedly engaging in deceptive schemes. Not surprisingly, conflict seems to swirl constantly about him. We will return to this theme of conflict in the next chapter. In this chapter, we focus our attention upon three topics: Isaac; Esau; Jacob's dream at Bethel.

Like so many, Isaac seems destined to be remembered in relation to others. He lives in the shadow of his father Abraham and son Jacob. Unfortunately, Isaac's similarities to his father appear in his decision to place his own security above that of his wife. Like his father, Isaac jeopardizes his wife Rebekah so that no harm may come to him. Like Abraham, God has to educate him through a foreign king! Isaac clearly strikes us as a rather passive figure. In his dealings with the Philistines, he repeatedly retreats rather than engages in strife. In contrast to his father who moved powerfully about the land rescuing the local inhabitants (Genesis 14), Isaac seems content simply to acquiesce to the inhabitants of the land. Though the text may be less than clear in its evaluation of Isaac's approach to conflict, it leaves no ambiguity about the blessings that come to him. As several scholars have noted, Isaac's life might be considered a living commentary on Psalm 37:

> Trust in the LORD, and do good;
>> so that you will live in the land, and enjoy security.
> Take delight in the LORD,
>> and he will give you the desires of your heart. . . .
> Be still before the LORD, and wait patiently for him;
>> do not fret over those who prosper in their way,
>> over those who carry out evil devices. . . .
> But the meek shall inherit the land,
>> and delight themselves in abundant prosperity. . . .
> The LORD knows the days of the blameless,
>> and their heritage will abide forever;
>> they are not put to shame in evil times,
>> in the days of famine they have abundance. . . .
> The salvation of the righteous is from the LORD;
>> he is their refuge in the time of trouble.

The LORD helps them and rescues them;
 he rescues them from the wicked, and saves them,
  because they take refuge in him (vv. 3-4,7,11,18-19,39-40)

■ What parallels in this passage do you see in your life?
■ What are the desires of your heart? Have you made them known to the Lord?
■ What does it mean to take refuge in the Lord? When has he rescued you?

Throughout, God blesses Isaac. His blessedness is visible to the very inhabitants who interact aggressively with him. Repeatedly we are told that Isaac is the beneficiary of Abraham's faithful obedience. If we are honest with ourselves, we all must acknowledge that we stand on the shoulders of those before us who lived in faithful obedience to the Lord. Like Isaac, the blessings in our lives often derive less from our own endeavors than from the faithful choices and actions of those who have gone before us. The life of Isaac wonderfully reminds us that even in our seeming weaknesses God faithfully wills to protect and care for us. Ironically, Isaac experiences a greater realization of the promise than his father Abraham!

In contrast to his father Isaac, Esau is truly a son who doesn't get it. Our first exposure to Esau makes clear that we have before us a person who takes lightly the precious promise made to his grandfather. Esau lives fully in the present. His immediate needs take precedence over any future realization of promises. Given his outlook, we are not surprised when he consistently makes poor choices. He sacrifices a promise for a meal; he marries local women who jeopardize the promise and make his parents' life miserable. Like Cain, in anger he seeks his brother's life (though Esau would surely consider his action "justifiable homicide"). Though a recipient of Abraham's blessing solely by his place in the family, his actions make him more akin to Ishmael than his father Isaac. Contention surrounds him; he (and his descendants) will ultimately live outside the land of promise. He will live "serving the younger brother" and away from the fertile land.

■ Have you known an Esau? Maybe you yourself have made similar choices? Can you think of specific situations that you would rather have chosen differently?

Jacob brings us up short. The favorite of his mother, he manifests far more her character than that of his passive father. He outmaneuvers his older brother from the day of his birth. Playing to his brother's weaknesses, he secures the birthright with nothing more than a meal. Later he will clinch that birthright with a blessing from his duped father. Strikingly, his only concern with his mother's deceptive plan is the punishment that might come from getting caught. When she willingly accepts any punishment that might accrue, he moves forward boldly. To allay his father's suspicions, he even brings God in on his deceit—he attributes the *speed* of his successful hunt to the Lord (27:20)!

Such behavior can only result in a life engulfed in conflict. Jacob's "successful" wresting of the blessing from his father puts his life in immediate danger. Esau, who lives fully in the present, plots his murder. Jacob must journey to survive. Only through the powerful presence of God can Jacob's journey for survival become a journey of faith. Such occurs at Bethel. Genesis 28:10-22 is for Jacob what 12:1-3 was for Abraham. At Bethel, Jacob comes fully into the presence of the God of his forefathers. *At that place,* God promises him presence, protection, and purpose. In the dream, Jacob receives an alternative vision for his life. The dream challenges him to refuse to let his shameful past dictate his future and embrace God's future for him. Jacob's journey for survival can become a journey of *faith.*

Although discussions of this text often spend an inordinate amount of time on its visual aspects, the true key to the passage resides in the divine speech (28:13-15). Similar to the Abraham narrative, God makes two promises to Jacob—he promises his *presence* ("I am with you") and his *protection* ("I will keep you"). These verses link Jacob's story with that of Abraham's story; the final verse details specifically Jacob's future.

■ Has a shameful past kept you from embracing the promise of God?

■ How have you made your struggle for survival a journey of faith?

Only the presence of God can transform an anxious exile into a promising future. If Psalm 37 captures the life of Isaac, Psalm 23 reverberates with language similar to God's promise to Jacob. Standing atop the staircase, God declares that he *will be with* Jacob and *keep him*. The first promises presence; the second, protection. Such language captures the heart of the gospel. Generations later God incarnate will promise presence and protection to his followers as he ascends to heaven: *"And remember, I am with you always, to the end of the age"* (Matthew 28:20).

■ What does God's promise of presence and protection mean to you?

Jacob's transformation is far from complete. Jacob's vow at Bethel is but the beginning of his "conversion." The Jacob we know to this point in the narrative grasps, deceives, and tricks. Conflict dominates his life, much the result of his own doing. For the first time in his life, Jacob is less a grasper than a receiver. Yet this is still *Jacob* leaving the land of promise for the old country. And yet, Jacob finds the word of God in his dream more convincing than his old world of fear and guilt. He manifests trust at this most crucial moment in his life. This supplanter becomes a promise bearer, changing an *ordinary place* into a *place of worship*. The presence and promise of God transforms Jacob; he begins his journey carrying deep commitments and decisions. As with the Abraham narrative, so in the Jacob cycle we encounter our own story. Like Jacob, at those moments when we most keenly recognize our vulnerability, often resulting from our own duplicity and failures, we may encounter the presence and protection of God. Like Jacob, the transformation of our future is rooted first and foremost in the divine willingness to promise presence and protection. Like Jacob, God's promising presence works to transform us from deceivers and tricksters into blessed promise bearers.

Genesis 28 also says something significant about God and

about worship. About God, Genesis 28 reminds us that God's transcendence is not compromised by his nearness. Scripture ably holds together the awe-inspiring majesty of God with his intimate presence and willingness to make himself accessible to us. Further, this awesome God willingly enters into relationship with less than savory characters. We find hope that through the promise of God's presence and protection we can be transformed to become what he has called us to be.

Regarding worship, Genesis 28 reminds us that "worship at a *place*" and "life as a *journey*" are not mutually exclusive. Although Jacob is embarking on a remarkable journey, a journey epitomized by the presence and protection of God, he will nonetheless return to this place (Bethel). Rightly understood, worship as place can provide our lives with order, assurance, and a tangible reminder of the presence and protection of God. It is wrongly understood when it is disconnected from the motif of journey. It is that disconnection to which Jesus addressed himself in the Gospel of John.

■ Explain how these verses from John's Gospel present us with the intimate linkage of worship as place and journey in the person of Jesus.

> *And the Word became flesh and lived [literally: tabernacled] among us, and we have seen his **glory**, the **glory** of a father's only son, full of grace and truth. . . .*
>
> *The woman said to him, "Sir, I see that you are a prophet. Our ancestors worshiped on this mountain, but you say that the place where people must worship is in Jerusalem." Jesus said to her, "Woman, believe me, the hour is coming when you will worship the Father neither on this mountain nor in Jerusalem. . . . But the hour is coming, and is now here, when the true worshipers will worship the Father in spirit and truth, for the Father seeks such as these to worship him"* (John 1:14; 4:19-21, 23, emphasis added).

CHAPTER 8

Living a Life of Conflict

(Genesis 29–36)

hat goes around comes around." As a new chapter in Jacob's life unfolds, irony reigns supreme. Jacob becomes a walking cliché. Jacob has safely escaped the angry threats and intended harm of a brother he deceived. To this point we have seen the endangered nature of his life in the land of promise, the reason for his hasty departure from that land, and the promise he receives as he exits the land. He will soon arrive at the apparently safe environs of his extended family. The remainder of the Jacob cycle recounts the life of the patriarch outside the land of promise and his return to that land. If we are reading the story for the first time, we might assume that Rebekah's family will surely take care of her favorite son. However, we soon learn that Jacob's life of deception and conflict has only just begun. The seeming safety of his mother's family will prove a *mixed blessing*. The blessings Jacob carries as the bearer of the promises to Abraham will prove a fascination to those living outside the land of promise. This section of the Jacob narrative reflects again a literary arrangement we have come to expect—ring composition. This time the reversal in story order matches the reversal in the relationship between Jacob and Laban. Ironically, at each end the narrative is *sealed with a kiss*.

OUTLINE 5 ■

(A) Jacob arrives in Haran (Laban) (29:1-14)
  (B) Jacob and Laban make a Contract (29:15-20)
   (C) Laban deceives Jacob (29:21-30)
    (D) The birth of Jacob's children (29:31–30:24)
   (C) Jacob tricks Laban (30:25-43)
  (B) Jacob and Laban dispute (31:17-24)
(A) Jacob departs from Laban (Haran) (30:43-54)

The second half of the Jacob cycle divides nicely into three major sections: Jacob and Laban outside the land of promise (chapters 29–31); Jacob and Esau at the margins of the land of promise (chapters 32–33); Jacob and his children "safely" back in the land of promise (chapters 34–35). Throughout the narrative wordplays and double entendre drive us to reread the narrative, remembering earlier episodes in the lives of the patriarchs, and anticipating later events in the next cycle of stories.

Jacob and Laban (Genesis 29–31)

When Jacob arrives in the vicinity of Haran, everything seems to fall into place. He stops at a well where shepherds are beginning to arrive to water their flocks. Apparently a large stone caps the well, and so the watering will not commence until a sufficient number of able-bodied shepherds have arrived to remove the large boulder. While we wait for the well to be uncapped, our thoughts return to an earlier scene in Genesis at a well. We recall the arrival of Abraham's servant at a well in search of a wife for his master's son (Genesis 24). The son (Jacob) of that wife (Rebekah) now comes to a well, causing us to wonder whether his story will play out similarly.

When he arrives Jacob inquires about his whereabouts. When he learns these shepherds are from Haran, he asks if they know his uncle Laban. They inform him that Laban's daughter is just now approaching the well. Upon seeing Rachel, Jacob, ever the opportunist ("heel grabber") single-handedly dislodges the stone from the mouth of the well! He next greets Rachel with a kiss and she races to tell her father of Jacob's arrival.

When Laban hears that his sister's son has arrived, he races to meet him. He greets him with a kiss and invites him to his house. Laban's response is most striking, *"surely you are my bone and my flesh!"* (29:14). The language is inviting; the rhetoric is powerful. We will later wonder whether Laban's rhetoric truly matches his behavior!

If Laban's opening exclamation intrigues us, the following scene is fraught with meaning and innuendo. After a month-long visit, Laban declares to Jacob, *"Because you are my kinsman, should you therefore serve me for nothing? Tell me, what shall your wages be?"* (29:15). Laban may be thinking wages; Jacob is thinking marriage. The opening transaction between Jacob and Laban begins innocently enough; however, we will soon discover that Jacob encounters in Laban a *wily adversary*. Jacob wants Rachel's hand in marriage. Laban, seemingly pleased with the plan, responds, *"It is better that I give her to you than that I give her to any other man; stay with me"* (29:19). They contract for seven years of service from Jacob in return for Rachel's hand in marriage. Seven years pass quickly when in love. At the end of seven years, Jacob is ready to consummate the marriage. Laban graciously offers to host a festival for the soon-to-be newlyweds. That night, Laban gives his daughter to Jacob. The next morning, Jacob awakens from the darkness to discover he has wed *not* Rachel, but her older sister Leah! Jacob the deceiver has been deceived!

We may wonder how one as cunning as Jacob could be so easily duped. Though Jacob apparently did not anticipate such an act on Laban's part, as readers we quickly return to the preceding paragraph and realize the seeds for such a move were already present! We were told that Laban had two daughters: Leah the older, and Rachel the younger. In their initial transaction, the "looks" of Rachel and Leah are mentioned. Rachel, like the favored women before her (Sarah and Rebekah), is "graceful and beautiful" (29:17). In contrast, Leah has "soft" eyes. The term in Hebrew is frustratingly ambiguous. Though numerous commentators suggest Leah suffered from "weak" eyesight, it seems preferable to understand that she had soft eyes. Such a reading suggests she either had beautiful eyes, or that her eyes did not "shine" (such being an attractive quality). Though we as moderns may wonder how Jacob could not have known he was marrying Leah, we must remember the attire of ancient Near Eastern women. The night of the wedding, Leah most likely would have been *hooded* with a heavy veil; only her eyes would have been exposed. In the darkness of the night, disguising identity would have come easily for a trickster like Laban. Just as Jacob had earlier deceived his father's eyes, so now the eyes of Leah cause his deception. The dialogue between the angered groom and the father-in-law intrigues us:

> *And Jacob said to Laban, "What is this you have done to me? Did I not serve with you for Rachel? Why then have you deceived me?" Laban said, "**This is not done in our country—giving the younger before the firstborn**" (29:25-26, emphasis added).*

Though Jacob may have stepped ahead of his *older* brother in the new country, he will not supplant the *older* sister in the *old* country.

Jacob's love for Rachel refuses to allow such a manipulative move to derail the marriage. Outwitted by his father-in-law, he now must submit to another contract for Rachel. The contract extends seven years; he receives Rachel in marriage at the end of the week-long festivities with his current bride Leah. The story pushes forward quickly. With a little more than a week passed, Jacob now finds himself responsible for two wives and two handmaids!

The following scene opens poignantly. Rachel shares not only *beauty* in common with the women of her new family (Sarah and Rebekah), she also tragically shares another trait—*barrenness*. Rachel the loved is barren; Leah the unloved (literally *hated*, clearly a term of contrast rather than emotion) is fertile. Though Leah is not chosen to bear the promise, she is (like Hagar before her) blessed by God. However, just as the barrenness of Sarah and the fertility of the handmaid Hagar generated strife in Abraham's household, so now Leah's fertility and Rachel's barrenness creates endless conflict.

Leah begins providing Jacob with heirs. Over the course of the next several years, Jacob's wives and their handmaids provide him with ten sons and one daughter. Leah first provides four sons. In jealousy Rachel gives her handmaid Bilhah to Jacob so that she might produce sons on her behalf. Bilhah bears two sons. Leah, no longer able to have children, responds by sending her handmaid Zilpah to Jacob, resulting in two more sons.

In a delightful, yet somewhat opaque scene, we learn of a *bargain* that Rachel and Leah strike. Just as their husband and father seem driven to outwit each other, so now Rachel and Leah jockey for position. Leah's oldest son Reuben finds mandrakes during the spring harvesting of the wheat. When Reuben brings them to his mother Leah, Rachel begs Leah to give her some of the mandrakes. (The mystique behind the mandrakes is less than clear. In Hebrew mandrakes were called "love apples" [*duda'im*, a play on the word for "love"—*dod*]. There is evidence ancient people may have thought mandrakes functioned as an aphrodisiac with powers of fertility.) Leah the unloved barters her son's mandrakes for a night with her estranged husband. Ironically, Rachel gets the mandrakes and Leah gets pregnant! Once again we are reminded that blessing has far more to do with God ("and God heeded Leah" [30:17]) than with manipulating circumstances. Leah is once again fertile. She bears two more sons and a daughter.

The mandrakes are ineffective, but God is not. "Then God remembered Rachel, and God heeded her and opened her womb. She conceived and bore a son" (30:22-23a). When all the dust settles (though soon to be stirred up), Jacob is the father of a *multitude*—eleven sons and one daughter. Throughout the narrative wordplays highlight the circumstances of the birth of each child. The following chart captures the significance of each child's birth.

Name of Child	Circumstances of Birth
Leah's First Round of Children	
Reuben—"See, a son" (*re'uben*)	"Because the Lord has *looked on my affliction*" [*ra'ah yhwh be`onyi*]
Simeon (*shim`on*)	"Because the Lord has *heard* [*shama`*] that I am hated"
Levi (*levi*)	"Now this time my husband will be *joined* [*yillaveh*] to me"
Judah (*yehudah*)	"This time *I will praise* ['*odeh*] the Lord"
Bilhah (Rachel's maid)	
Dan (*dan*)	"God *has judged me*" [*dananni*]
Naphtali (*naphtali*)	"With *mighty wrestlings* [*naphtule 'elohim niphtalti*] I have wrestled with my sister"
Zilpah (Leah's maid)	
Gad (*gad*)	"*Good fortune*" [*bagad*]
Asher ('*asher*)	"*Happy am I*" [*be'ashri*]
Leah's Second Round of Children	
Issachar (*yissaschar*)	"God has given me *my hire*" [*sakari*]
Zebulun (*zebulun*)	"God has endowed me with a good dowry; now my husband *will honor me*" [*yizbeleni*]
Dinah (only daughter)	(no wordplay)
Rachel's Child	
Joseph (*yoseph*)	"God has *taken away* ['*asaph*] my reproach… may the Lord *add to me* [*yoseph*] another son!"

As this scene closes, our experience with the promise to Abraham has shifted considerably. To this point, the land portion of the promise typically seemed secure. Though Abraham and Isaac experienced brief hiatuses outside the land, the bulks of their lives were spent within the land of promise. Fulfilling the descendants' portion of the promise typically loomed ominously on the horizon. By Genesis 30, Abraham's descendants are proliferating; however, the land of promise is far removed from the bearer of the promise. Jacob now seeks to remedy that shortcoming. He goes to his father-in-law Laban requesting permission to return to his homeland. He seeks no wages other than the "receipt" from his original contract—his wives (and children).

Laban informs Jacob that he has learned by *divination* that his own success is the result of Jacob's presence. Jacob is indeed the bearer of blessings. Laban is unwilling to let Jacob depart. He counters by offering Jacob a share of his wealth, a wealth ironically gained because of Jacob! Laban duped Jacob once; Jacob will not allow it to happen again. Jacob persists; he argues he must begin securing a future for his own family. (We are almost left with the impression that should Jacob leave, his family and any property accruing to them would remain with Laban.) Jacob offers Laban a deal too good to refuse. Jacob will take nothing of value from Laban; he will continue to care for Laban's flock, taking only those goats and sheep that have no value—the runts and those that produce mediocre wool (speckled and spotted).

Laban immediately agrees, and secretly implements a plan to outmaneuver Jacob once more. Laban removes all the valueless goats he has just given Jacob, placing them three-days distant from the main flock. This time Jacob will not be outmaneuvered. Apparently understanding animal husbandry, Jacob engages in selective breeding and soon secures for himself a massive flock. What Laban had learned by divination is true—Jacob is the source of his blessings! Jacob becomes rich; he soon possesses not only large flocks, but also slaves, camels, and donkeys.

Conflict constantly surrounds Jacob. Just as his favoritism for Rachel brought conflict into his personal life, so his wealth now brings conflict into his professional life. The sons of Laban (previously unmentioned) attempt to turn the tables against their brother-in-law. They argue to their father that Jacob is becoming rich at Laban's expense! (Their complaint somewhat matches Esau's earlier complaint to his father.) Jacob knows he must act quickly and decisively. To this point, Jacob's success seems solely the result of his strategic breeding practices. However, when he gathers his family together, he informs them that an angel of the Lord revealed to him the true reason for the successful mating of the flocks. The God he met at Bethel is indeed fulfilling his promises. Jacob is blessed and is a blessing to those around him.

However, God is now calling him to return to the land of promise. Knowing his departure will create conflict, Jacob decides to leave while Laban and his sons are themselves three-days distant! The response of Leah and Rachel is telling, and helps us fill in the gaps. They reply:

> "Is there any portion or inheritance left to us in our father's house? Are we not regarded by him as foreigners? For he has sold us, and he has been using up the money given for us. All the property that God has taken away from our father belongs to us and to our children; now then, do whatever God has said to you" (31:14-15).

These daughters of Laban realize their father sold them (the language of slavery) for work (not silver) from which he became rich. However, instead of placing it in the dowry belonging to them and their children, he has selfishly spent it on himself. The text makes sure we keep the entire story before us. Through wordplay, it captures the drama of the event. Laban (*laban*) negotiates for the *white* (*laban*) goats; Jacob peels back the bark of the *poplar branches* (*leban-ot*) and exposes the *white* (*laban*) (30:37); Jacob's wives now claim the wealth for themselves and their *children* (*lebanenu*) (31:16).

Though exiting quickly and with a three-day lead, the pace of a large family and livestock is no match for Laban and his compatriots. Laban overtakes Jacob and his entourage seven days later at the edge of the land of promise—the region of Gilead (the northeastern border of Canaan). Laban feigns hurt feelings and accuses Jacob of duplicity. Laban disingenuously declares that Jacob's flight denied him the opportunity to provide his daughters and grandchildren a lavish going away party! We cannot help but wonder what might have gone through Jacob's mind at the thought of experiencing another festival hosted by Laban! More importantly, Laban charges Jacob with theft. However, the theft is not livestock, but household gods. Laban claims Jacob has stolen his *teraphim* (small figurines often kept in a dwelling to protect it from harm). Jacob, not knowing Rachel confiscated the statuettes, professes innocence of any wrongdoing and invites Laban to search the camp.

The die is cast. Surely an extensive search of the camp will expose Laban's idols. However, a search of Leah's tent and the tent of the two maids uncovers nothing. When Laban enters Rachel's tent, he begins to *feel about* (*mashash*) for his figurines, just as Jacob's father Isaac had earlier *felt* (*mashash*) his son to determine his identity. In a move of genius, Rachel outmaneuvers her father. She places the *teraphim* ignominiously under her camel saddle; she then begs her father not to make her move, since she is suffering from her menstrual period.

Jacob, not privy to Rachel's theft, *rightly* expresses outrage at the conclusion of Laban's search. He pointedly argues that throughout his tenure with Laban he consistently acted in good faith. He took nothing from Laban; in fact, he even covered Laban's financial losses out of his own pocket. Jacob's speech is dramatic:

> *Then Jacob became angry, and upbraided Laban. Jacob said to Laban, "What is my offense? What is my sin, that you have hotly pursued me? Although you have felt about through all my goods, what have you found of all your household goods? Set it here before my kinsfolk and your kinsfolk, so that they may decide between us two. These twenty years I have been with you; your ewes and your female goats have not miscarried, and I have not eaten the rams of your flocks. That which was torn by wild beasts I did not bring to you; I bore the loss of it myself; of my hand you required it, whether stolen by day or stolen by night. It was like this with me: by day the heat consumed me, and the cold by night, and my sleep fled from my eyes. These twenty years I have been in your house; I served you fourteen years for your two daughters, and six years for your flock, and you have changed my wages ten times.* **If the God of my father, the God of Abraham and the Fear of Isaac, had not been on my side, surely now you would have sent me away empty-handed.** *God saw my affliction and the labor of my hands, and rebuked you last night"* (31:36-42, emphasis added).

We never learn the motivation for Rachel's theft. Speculation abounds. Some suggest Rachel remained an avid worshiper of these (now) foreign gods. (Later Jacob will call his family to abandon their former gods and embrace the God of his father Abraham and Isaac [35:2].) Alternately, several suggest Rachel's (dis)regard for her father's gods is more clearly reflected in her symbolic actions. By taking these figurines, she implicitly demonstrated that these gods were powerless in the presence of the God Jacob now called her to worship. They were unable to prevent their own departure from Haran. Further, her sitting upon these gods during her menstrual period surely demonstrated a disdain and willful lack of respect for these religious objects.

While Rachel's intent may be unclear, the outcome of Jacob's departure is not. Laban, realizing he is powerless to prevent Jacob's return to Canaan, mounts a final feeble attempt to claim responsibility for Jacob's blessedness. Rightly distrustful of each other, the two tricksters now enter into a covenant. To seal the covenant and preserve the memory of this momentous occasion, they erect a pillar and mound up stones about it in a large heap. Laban the Aramean names the place *Jegar-sahadutha* (Aramaic = "heap of witness"); Jacob the Hebrew names it *Galeed* (Hebrew = "heap of witness"). The pillar Jacob names *Mizpah* (Hebrew = "watchpost"). They agree not to invade each other's territory for harm. The following morning, Laban kisses his grandchildren and daughters and offers them a parting blessing. The stage is set for Jacob's re-entry into the land of promise.

Jacob and Esau (Genesis 32–33)

In many ways, the Jacob narrative is neatly framed by Jacob's exit and re-entry into Canaan. He flees to escape his brother's wrath; he re-enters to escape the turmoils of life with his uncle Laban. Conflict finds Jacob wherever he goes. Having just concluded a peace treaty with Laban, Jacob now plans for a potential encounter with his estranged brother Esau. In his preparations for this meeting, we again meet Jacob's dual nature. He plans, prays, and plans again!

As Jacob plans for his meeting with Esau, he first meets angels. Just as he encountered angels of the Lord ascending and descending the staircase at Bethel on his departure from Canaan (Genesis

28), so now he encounters angels as he re-enters. He appropriately names the location of the encounter—*Double camp (Mahanaim)*. Jacob sends messengers ahead to initiate a peace treaty with his brother. Jacob seeks favor from Esau. The messengers return with an ominous message. Esau is approaching with 400 men; the messengers and Jacob clearly assume these men have militaristic intentions. Jacob shrewdly divides his entourage into two companies, thinking that perhaps one will escape even if the other is captured or slaughtered.

Jacob next prays. If there is a moment of righteousness in Jacob's life, we find it here. In contrast to his earlier prayer at Bethel that contained an element of contractual language, Jacob here acknowledges that his wealth and blessings are entirely the manifestation of God's graciousness—he is completely undeserving. Jacob honestly admits his fear at the arrival of his brother. He has no recourse other than to seek God's continued favor.

> *And Jacob said, "O God of my father Abraham and God of my father Isaac, O LORD who said to me, 'Return to your country and to your kindred, and I will do you good,' I am not worthy of the least of all the steadfast love and all the faithfulness that you have shown to your servant, for with only my staff I crossed this Jordan; and now I have become two companies. Deliver me, please, from the hand of my brother, from the hand of Esau, for I am afraid of him; he may come and kill us all, the mothers with the children. Yet you have said, 'I will surely do you good, and make your offspring as the sand of the sea, which cannot be counted because of their number.'" (32:9-12).*

The stage is set for the reunion of the siblings. Jacob implements one final strategic move. He separates out from his abundant possessions a substantial gift of livestock for Esau. He provides explicit instructions to the attendants herding this large gift. As they approach Esau in waves, they are each to announce that these animals are gifts from his brother Jacob.

Anticipating an extremely difficult tomorrow, Jacob assists his family and livestock ford the Jabbok River. Having gotten the entire retinue across safely, Jacob camps alone at the riverbank. That night Jacob was surely fixated upon the almost certain conflict with Esau that was coming the next day. However, at the Jabbok (*yabboq*), a most unusual event transpires. Jacob finds himself assaulted by a stranger and locked in a mighty wrestling (*ye'abeq*) match throughout the night! Though the text never identifies the assailant as God, Jacob is certain that such is the identity of his opponent. Surely Jacob must have wrestled in bewilderment. This God who had protected him throughout his stay outside the land of promise was now battling him as he sought to re-enter that same land! Like Jacob, we expect God to oppose the manipulative and self-centered and to protect the penitent. Here God seemingly operates in reverse!

Jacob proves a worthy adversary. The two combatants struggle throughout the night, apparently with no clear winner. As dawn is breaking, the assailant seeks release. Jacob refuses; he will not release his grip without a blessing. Jacob's response is astonishing, for if this is truly God, Jacob must surely know he cannot see God and survive! In response to Jacob's request for a *blessing*, he receives a *new name*. His opponent renames this "heel-grabber" *Israel* (most likely—"struggles with God"). With a new name, Jacob takes another approach. He now asks the name of his assailant. To that request, the opponent refuses, but now grants the blessing he earlier sought. Jacob's blessing comes at a costly price. His adversary dislocates his hip; Jacob will begin his march toward his imminent conflict with Esau crippled! Remarkably, Jacob/Israel has changed. As he limps toward his family, he talks not about his injury, nor expresses bewilderment at this attack from God, but marvels that he has *seen God face to face* and lived! Jacob finds grace in this most unexpected moment and place. Just as he earlier renamed the ancient site Luz to Bethel after his encounter with God, so he now names the site of his re-entry into the land of promise Penuel/Peniel ("face of God").

If Jacob's all-night wrestling match surprises us, the following scene continues the surprise. Jacob moves to the front of his "battalion," a force consisting of women, children, and livestock! As he comes into range of Esau, he bows himself to the ground seven times. When Esau sees Jacob, he runs to him, embraces him, and begins to kiss him and weep. If this is a battle strategy, it is most unusual! Where we expect conflict to occur we encounter reconciliation. Esau has long rid himself of his anger and desire to kill Jacob.

Esau expresses that he has no need of gifts from Jacob. The scene is striking—two estranged brothers attempting to outgive the other. Jacob offers gifts; Esau offers his 400 men as protective escorts! Perhaps no moment is more poignant than when Jacob acknowledges that seeing his estranged brother Esau is like "*seeing the face of God—since you have received me with such favor*" (33:10).

The scene closes with an amicable parting. Esau returns across the river to the region of Seir. Jacob slowly makes his way to Succoth, so named for the "booths" (*Sukkoth*) he constructs there. He eventually makes his way to Shechem. At Shechem he purchases a plot of land from the residents of the area (the sons of Hamor) and pitches his tent on the site. Like his grandfather Abraham, he builds an altar, claiming the land for the God of his fathers. He embraces his new name with this altar; he names it *El-Elohe-Israel* ("God, God of Israel").

Jacob "Safely" Back in the Land of Promise (Genesis 34–35)

Surprise continues as we move into Genesis 34–35. Just as we experience a major reversal in expectations when Jacob and Esau finally meet, so a reversal in expectations surfaces in Genesis 34. Genesis 34 narrates a tragic episode in the life of Jacob's only daughter—Dinah. (The remainder of the book of Genesis will focus entirely upon events in the lives of Jacob's numerous sons.)

As the scene opens, life seems peaceful for the co-inhabitants of the region of Shechem. The level of safety in the region apparently allows young women to move about with no thought of harm. Dinah, the lone daughter surrounded by males, journeys forth to visit with the women of the region. However, tragedy occurs. Whereas the earlier encounter of Jacob and Esau moved from presumed hostility to reconciliation, this narrative moves from presumed peace and security to violent rape. Shechem, the royal son of the man who sold Jacob his property, seizes Dinah and rapes her. However, unlike Amnon, the later Davidic prince who rapes his sister and then finds his victim repulsive, Shechem falls in love with his victim.

When Jacob hears that his daughter has been violated, he does nothing. Apparently he is awaiting the return of her brothers from their chores with the livestock. As the news of this outrage spreads,

Jacob finds himself immersed in a most murky and ethical dilemma. On the one hand, his sons express outrage and clearly intend to inflict revenge. On the other hand, Hamor, the father of Shechem, seeks the hand of the defiled Dinah in marriage to his son. Hamor, recognizing his son's love for this woman he has violated, extends an open-ended contract to Jacob. Earlier Abraham offered a seemingly extravagant price to the Canaanites for a piece of property to honor his deceased wife Sarah; now a Canaanite offers the descendant of Abraham open access to the land, free trade, and marriage contracts.

Interestingly, the ensuing negotiations take place not between Jacob and Hamor, but between the sons of Jacob and Shechem and his father. They counter the offer with a demand that all the residents of the city of Shechem undergo circumcision. Circumcision, that act that originally signified Abraham's total commitment to the call and claim of God upon his life, is now exploited by these sons in an act of deception. The Shechemites are duped. They regard the sons of Jacob as friendly negotiators. They also silently seem to ponder the benefits that will come to them from this contractual arrangement with a people who are "blessed" (34:23—"*Will not their livestock, their property, and all their animals be ours?*") The events move forward at a rapid pace. While the men of Shechem are still healing, Jacob's sons Simeon and Levi enter the city and slaughter the recovering males. The remainder of the brothers later come and plunder the city, taking *livestock, women, and children*. The men of Shechem will not reap the benefits from this transaction!

Jacob now enters the fray. Though he chides his sons Simeon and Levi, his motivation seems primarily rooted in fear from the hostile response he may receive from the surrounding Canaanite neighbors. For this there will be no peaceful resolution; violence begets violence. His sons are unrepentant. They show little concern for any repercussions their activities may bring; their sole concern has been to avenge the disgraceful treatment of their sister. The interactions of the patriarchs and the residents of Canaan intrigue us. Abraham seemingly moves through the land fearlessly, manifesting fear only when he must exit the land of promise. He on one occasion even rescues the inhabitants of the land and refuses any compensation for his endeavors. Isaac seemingly interacts timidly with the inhabitants. He repeatedly moves to release tense moments, yet at a most strategic moment enters into a mutually beneficial pact with the Philistines. Jacob seems thoroughly pragmatic. He calculates the response of the Canaanites to any action he might take in the case with Dinah. Though Jacob is fearful, his sons manifest no concern for later complications that their actions may produce. They fearlessly and brutally exact revenge, a revenge seemingly out of proportion to the original act of violence. Their actions set the stage for the conflict that will surround the cohabitation of the descendants of Abraham and the residents of Canaan throughout the remainder of the Bible.

God resolves Jacob's fears. He instructs him to move from Shechem to Bethel. However, this time Bethel will serve not as the launching pad for Jacob's hasty exit from the land of promise, but as the focal point for Jacob, *and all his household*, to enter into a much more important relationship. At Bethel Jacob and his family will again experience fully the promise God made generations earlier to Abraham. Jacob rightly understands the momentous nature of this return to Bethel. He calls his entire household to scrap the foreign idols and images they have been transporting. Rachel will no longer carry the teraphim of her father. Jacob takes these "treasures" and buries them at Shechem. At Bethel, God renews the Abrahamic promises with Jacob.

> *God appeared to Jacob again when he came from Paddan-aram, and he blessed him. God said to him, "Your name is Jacob; no longer shall you be called Jacob, but Israel shall be your name." So he was called Israel. God said to him, "I am God Almighty: be fruitful and multiply; a nation and a company of nations shall come from you, and kings shall spring from you. The land that I gave to Abraham and Isaac I will give to you, and I will give the land to your offspring after you." Then God went up from him at the place where he had spoken with him. Jacob set up a pillar in the place where he had spoken with him, a pillar of stone; and he poured out a drink offering on it, and poured oil on it* (35:9-14).

The promises seem complete. The promise bearer is again safely ensconced in the land of promise; the descendants of Abraham are numerous. The Jacob cycle closes with three death reports and a concluding genealogy of Esau's descendants. We hear of the death of Rebekah's nurse Deborah, the peaceful death of Isaac in old age, and the death of Rachel during a most difficult childbirth (the birth of Benjamin/Benoni). God grants the request Rachel uttered at the birth of his first child Joseph. She prayed that God would grant her another child, but it comes at a high price—her life.

Finding Ourselves in Genesis 29–36

The Jacob narrative is certainly no "they lived happily ever after" story. Conflict surrounds Jacob from beginning to end. The elder may serve the younger, but not without turmoil. *Israel* (the descendants) will emerge out of the conflict between Rachel and Leah, just as *Israel* (the patriarch Jacob) will emerge out of conflict with God. Jacob initially experiences conflict with his brother Esau, later with his uncle Laban, and ultimately with his God! Some of that conflict will result from his own making, some of that conflict will come to him uninvited, through all of the conflict he will move closer to the God of his fathers Abraham and Isaac.

Jacob flees the wrath of Esau only to have to go "toe-to-toe" with another relative. Though his entrance into his mother's former house begins innocently enough, warning signs quickly surface. Laban recognizes the benefits that accrue with Jacob's presence. He seals a marriage contract that Jacob only later tragically realizes leaves him with nothing other than his wives. His children and possessions must be negotiated. Laban bargains hard and ruthlessly. Through it all we see the slow transformation of Jacob from one who aggressively grasps for everything he can get to one who recognizes that his belongings come from One who gives to him freely and faithfully.

■ When have you taken two steps forward and three steps back? When have you felt as though you were wasting your time?

Not surprisingly, the conflict is often rooted in partiality and the favored treatment of one person to the neglect of another. Isaac favors Esau; Rebekah favors Jacob. Sibling animosity and conflict result. Jacob later favors Rachel at the expense of Leah. Rachel jealously wishes she could have the children that seem to come so effortlessly to Leah. Leah desperately longs for the affection of her husband that Rachel receives. Frustrated by her inability to have a child, Rachel blames Jacob. In response, Jacob retorts, *"Am I in the place of God?"* (30:2). Genesis 3 has been turned on its head! Where Adam blamed his wife, Rachel now blames her husband!

Though Jacob may at times appall us with his duplicitous maneuvers and devious schemes, we may also take hope. For if we are honest, we are often more like Jacob than not. Like Jacob, God often blesses us in spite of ourselves. Repeatedly we meet in Jacob mixed motives and less than honorable actions. In one and the same moment, he can devise elaborate plans and pray. He can operate from seemingly purely pragmatic motives while simultaneously acknowledging the Lord as the sole source of his life and wealth. We are not surprised when Jacob becomes the sole patriarch who experiences a name change, and yet continues to be called by both names! He may now be Israel, but Jacob is still very much a part of his identity. The life of Jacob vividly reminds us that, though *conversion* may occur quickly, *sanctification* is a lifelong process.

■ When have you been a victim of favoritism? Have you ever shown partiality? What conflicts resulted from either type of situations?

Two moments define Jacob. They occur at pivotal moments in his life. The first occurs at the moment of his exit from the land of promise (Genesis 28). At Bethel, Jacob encounters the God who promises him presence and protection. Jacob will not journey alone. He may be leaving his family and moving in reverse, but a faithful and loving God accompanies him. The second defining moment occurs at his re-entry into the land of promise (Genesis 32). At the Jabbok River, Jacob's life changes forever. What Genesis 22 (the binding of Isaac) is to the Abraham cycle, the wrestling match at the Jabbok is to the Jacob cycle. Several scholars have noted that this text is worthy of a Rembrandt; one has quipped that it is also as enigmatic as the Mona Lisa!

Genesis 32 is to the Jacob narrative what Genesis 22 is to the Abraham cycle. This passage is equally enigmatic (if not more so). Within the larger context, Jacob, bearer of the Abrahamic promises, is returning home. The promise to Abraham is about to re-enter the promised land. However, it is the immediate context that provides the drama and poignancy for the narrative, for in this land of promise resides Esau. Jacob the blessed must deal finally with the anger and threats of his brother Esau. In Jacob's preparations for this meeting we meet again the dual nature of Jacob. On the one hand, Jacob is shrewd, calculating, and cautious. He thinks strategically about how and in what order he (and those for whom he is responsible) will meet Esau. His language may possess elements of barter and manipulation. On the other hand, we encounter the changed Jacob, the Jacob who appeals to the Lord (32:9-12). The text notes these two sides to Jacob—he plans, he prays, and he plans!

At that moment when we are poised for this dramatic encounter between estranged (and potentially hostile) siblings, a most unexpected encounter occurs. On the eve of his encounter with Esau, Jacob encounters none other than the God who met him as he departed the promised land! The scene is startling and laced with irony. The God who has stood with Jacob throughout his tenure in Mesopotamia now stands in his way as antagonist! Amazingly, when Jacob later encounters Esau, he will experience reconciliation and an invitation to community. In fact, his encounter with Esau will be *like seeing God* (33:10)! Having experienced the awesomeness of God manifested in protection and blessing (Genesis 28), he now experiences the divine presence in conflict and opposition. An ironic reversal occurs—Jacob experiences God acting as he presumed Esau would act and Esau acting toward him as he had previously experienced God!

Frederick Buechner has a marvelous meditation on this passage entitled "The Magnificent Defeat" (or alternately he calls it "The Crippling Victory"). This suggests that Jacob neither wins nor loses! Rather, he and God wrestle to a draw. The text suggests this in several ways. On the one hand, Jacob crosses the river the following morning limping with a dislocated hip (permanent or temporarily disabling?). On the other hand, he has his assailant in such a grip that the assailant asks to be released before daybreak. Given the opponent's divine identity, releasing the hold before daylight is paramount, since in the Old Testament one cannot see the face of God and live! Amazingly, Jacob seems willing to risk even death to receive a blessing! Later Moses will experience a similarly enigmatic divine "attack" as he re-enters Egypt (Exodus 4:24-26). These texts serve to remind us that our lives and futures are not controlled by the human obstacles in our road, but by the God who stands before us, behind us, and beside us! Jacob's future was never more secure than when he limped forth to meet his brother. To paraphrase a later declaration of Jesus, *"do not fear the one who simply has the power of life and death, fear the One who can ultimately destroy"* (Matthew 10:28). As unsettling as it may seem, the narrative of Jacob reminds us that often before God fights for us, he often has to fight *against us*. At times we only come to recognize the true source of our blessings and life when we experience God's *crippling* touch. In this moment we not only see Jacob's dual nature, but the dual stance of God. As Christians, like Jacob we acknowledge this dual nature when we *pray—"lead us not into temptation, but deliver us from evil"* (Matthew 6:13).

The dialogue between Jacob and his assailant throbs with drama. In the first two exchanges the *man* speaks, in the third Jacob speaks. (Though the assailant throughout is identified as a man, Jacob knows more is at stake.) The *man* first requests that Jacob release him; in response Jacob asks for a blessing. The *man* then asks Jacob his name and gives him a new name! Jacob reciprocates by asking his assailant his name, at which point Jacob receives his requested blessing! The language is telling. The *man* acknowledges that Jacob has *prevailed*; Jacob at daybreak acknowledges he has *"seen God face to face, and yet my life is preserved."*

Although struggle dominates the text under consideration, Jacob could not struggle (and *prevail*) if God did not choose willingly to enter the struggle. In this way Genesis 32 may relate theologically to Genesis 15 (God's incredible willingness to make himself vulnerable to Abraham). From a Christian viewpoint, this text may allow us to marvel again at the utter magnitude of the incarnation and the cross. Like Genesis 32, in the incarnation and cross we come face to face with both the power of God and the apparent willingness of God to manifest that power in seeming weakness! Whereas human power eschews any notions of weakness and vulnerability, divine power manifests itself in ways always appropriate to the situation.

Second, it is in the midst of this seeming weakness that we, like Jacob, experience what only God as God can give—blessing! Jacob becomes our teacher at this point. While holding this "man" in his grip, a position that would intimate the weakness of his assailant's position, Jacob seeks a blessing, something that only one with power could bestow. Recognizing this allows us to make sense of the subsequent scene with Esau. In Genesis 33, Jacob presents himself to Esau not as a victim of divine capriciousness and malice, but as a recipient of gracious beneficence.

Third, Jacob's subsequent characterization of God and his beneficence is most striking. Note the meeting and dialogue of Jacob and Esau:

> Esau said, "What do you mean by all this company that I met?" Jacob answered, "To find favor with my lord." But Esau said, "I have enough, my brother; keep what you have for yourself." Jacob said, "No, please; if I find favor with you, then accept my present from my hand; **for truly to see your face is like seeing the face of God**—since you have received me with such favor. Please accept my gift that is brought to you, **because God has dealt graciously with me, and because I have everything I want.**" So he urged him, and he took it (33:8-11, emphasis added).

■ Give personal examples of your "wrestling matches" with God. What did you learn about God's control of the future?

Centuries later, two brothers came to Jesus with a bold request. They sought key positions in the soon-to-come kingdom of God. Though the disciples were offended (most likely because James and John had beaten them to the request!), Jesus simply opened their eyes to a larger vision of the road that lay before them. Like Jacob at the Jabbok, they encountered that day a God who does the surprising and unexpected. Jesus turned their eyes in an entirely different direction.

> But Jesus said to them, "You do not know what you are asking. . . . When the ten heard this, they began to be angry with James and John. So Jesus called them and said to them, "You know that among the Gentiles those whom they recognize as their rulers lord it over them, and their great ones are tyrants over them. But it is not so among you; but whoever wishes to become great among you must be your servant, and whoever wishes to be first among you must be slave of all. **For the Son of Man came not to be served but to serve, and to give his life a ransom for many**" (Mark 10:38,41-45, emphasis added).

■ When has God given you the seemingly opposite answer to your requests? How have you responded?

Such captures the dual nature of God, and the dual nature of the disciples he calls to be followers.

Though Jacob may at times appall us with his duplicitous maneuvers and devious schemes, we may also take hope. For if we are honest, we are often more like Jacob than not. Like Jacob, God often blesses us in spite of ourselves. Repeatedly we meet in Jacob mixed motives and less than honorable actions. In one and the same moment, he can devise elaborate plans and pray. He can operate from seemingly purely pragmatic motives while simultaneously acknowledging the Lord as the sole source of his life and wealth.

CHAPTER 9

Life In and Out of the Pit

(Genesis 37–41)

enesis 37 begins simply—*"Jacob settled in the land where his father had lived as an alien, the land of Canaan. This is the story of the family of Jacob."* The chapter might more fittingly open with the proverb from Ezekiel—"the fathers have eaten sour grapes, and the children's teeth are set on edge" (Ezekiel 18:2 RSV). The final chapters of Genesis transfer us to a new generation of promise bearers. From one vantage point, Genesis 37–50 narrates the lives of the children of Jacob. From another vantage point, the final chapters of Genesis narrate the events in the lives of Jacob's children from the vantage of the favorite child—Joseph. Genesis 37–50 is rightly called the Joseph cycle.

The Joseph narrative sits strategically between the Jacob cycle of stories and the book of Exodus. Though these chapters are important in their own right, they also prepare us for the events that will transpire when all the descendants of Israel find themselves in Egypt. These chapters provide the bridge between Canaan and Egypt.

Throughout the Jacob cycle we were engulfed in conflict. Jacob experienced conflict in his own relationships with his brother Esau, his uncle Laban, and his God. He watched as his wives struggled with each other for his love and attention. In Genesis 37–50, that conflict continues. However, it now advances to the next generation. Jacob's children will struggle for position and pride of place. Animosity and jealousy will characterize the relationship between Joseph and his brothers.

Though conflict is present throughout much of the Joseph narrative, another theme takes pride of place. Throughout the narratives concerning Abraham, Isaac, and Jacob, God appears often and in various manifestations. At times he sends messengers; at other times he comes himself. He appears verbally and visually. However, when we enter Genesis 37–50, God becomes virtually absent! God makes no appearances and enters into conversation with no one. As we move with Joseph from one dangerous episode to the next, we cannot help but ask, "Where is God?" We must be clear. God has not been forgotten; Joseph and the narrator mention God several times. However, God does not seem *visibly* active in the affairs of Joseph and his family. We suggest that the seeming *hiddenness* of God represents the major theme of the Joseph narrative, a theme we will treat in detail in the final chapter.

Though Jacob has twelve sons and one daughter, the focal point of the remainder of Genesis concerns the favorite son (Joseph) of the favorite wife (Rachel). Earlier the text has told us brief episodes in the lives of Leah's first three sons. Reuben, the firstborn, presumptuously took his father's concubine Bilhah and slept with her (35:22). Simeon and Levi masterminded the retaliatory vendetta against the men of Shechem over the rape of their sister Dinah. In Genesis 38, we will hear of a dramatic episode in the life of Leah's fourth son Judah. However, the bulk of the materials in this final section of Genesis concerns Joseph; the lives and fortunes of Jacob's family are caught in the life and (mis)fortunes of this favored son.

Joseph the Dreamer (Genesis 37)

Our first encounter with Joseph does not endear him to us. Just as our first experience with Jacob left us with the impression of a deceptive trickster willing to do most anything to put himself in an advantageous position, so now we meet his favored son who seems willing to do most anything to aggravate and anger his siblings. The Joseph we meet in Genesis 37 is a spoiled brat. He tattles on one set of brothers; he aggravates the others with his dreams of superiority.

Joseph and his brothers know only too well his favored status—he wears it daily! Joseph is the sole possessor of a lavish coat from his father. His coat, traditionally called a "coat of many colors," is more likely a coat with long sleeves (expensive in the ancient Near East) or a variegated coat with some type of elaborate embroidery. With each appearance, the brothers are reminded of their second-class status in the eyes of their father. Joseph exploits the situation. Though sent to function as a "helper" to his brothers Dan, Naphtali, Gad, and Asher, he voluntarily files a bad report about them to his father.

Already despised by his brothers, Joseph exacerbates the situation by detailing his dreams. In his first dream, he and his brothers are binding sheaves of grain in the field. Suddenly, his brothers' sheaves of grain gather round his sheaf and bow down.

Joseph's narration needs no interpretation for his brothers. They clearly understand his intent—he is superior to them and they should acknowledge such. His second dream further elevates his status. He dreams that the sun, moon, and *eleven* stars bow down to him. When he divulges this dream, even his father Jacob is offended. Jacob publicly rebukes his son, but we are told he internally continued to ponder the meaning of the dream. (In the ancient world, it was often assumed that a key criterion to distinguish idle dreams from dreams with a larger significance was whether a dream came singly or in pairs. Only dreams that occurred in pairs were considered to carry a larger significance.)

Given the level of animosity between Joseph and his brothers, Jacob's next move is surprising. Jacob sends his favored son to check on his other brothers. Having voluntarily filed one negative report on his siblings, Jacob sends his son to discover the "well-being" (*shalom*) of his (other?) brothers (37:14). The language is striking—our last report on Jacob's other sons informs us that they hated Joseph and could not speak *peaceably* (*shalom*) to him (v. 4). Since the descendants of Abraham are pastoral nomads, the availability of good pasturage determines their movements. They are quite distant from the southern region of Hebron, having moved northward to the more promising pastures surrounding Shechem. Joseph travels the highway north to Shechem; however, when he arrives, he learns his brothers have migrated again and are now pasturing at Dothan.

When the brothers see Joseph approaching, their hatred takes control. They plot his death. From their standpoint, this presumptuous dreamer should experience a nightmarish end to his life. They determine to kill him and dispose of the body in a nearby pit. Their declaration is haunting: "*Come now, let us kill him . . . **and we shall see what will become of his dreams**" (51:20). They will later tell their father that a wild animal must have killed his son. Reuben, the firstborn, joins the fray. He counters with a proposal that they first throw Joseph into the pit, and then later determine their next move. Reuben's proposal is ingeniously ambiguous. To the brothers, it may suggest an initial terrorizing of this hated brother with the delayed gratification of killing him. However, the text informs us that Reuben intends to rescue this hated brother and dispatch him to his father at his first opportunity.

Reuben's plan initially prevails, but ultimately fails. Joseph is thrown into his first pit; it will not be his last. Ironically, the brothers toss him in a pit and sit down to share a meal. (Later Joseph and his brothers will share a meal in Egypt in reverse positions of power.) While eating, the brothers (apparently minus Reuben) spy a passing caravan. A new idea enters their minds. Killing Joseph simply brings the satisfaction of removing the aggravation permanently from their midst. Selling their brother to a slave caravan rids them of this pest while simultaneously enriching them! The transaction is made and Joseph gone when Reuben returns to the pit. When he discovers the deal his brothers struck, he panics. Realizing the *grief* this will cause his father, he himself grieves. He tears his own clothes. His brothers, however, seem little concerned about their father's grief; they think only strategically about their father's potential *anger*. Reuben may tear his own clothes; they will tear the clothing of the brother they have just sold. They shred the favored robe and soil it with goat's blood.

Reuben knows his father well. Upon returning to their father, they display the torn and bloodstained coat. Though they feign ignorance of its identity, Jacob immediately recognizes the coat and draws the conclusion the brothers intended. His favorite son has died gruesomely at the jaws of a wild animal. Jacob descends into deep grief over the death of Rachel's firstborn. Like his firstborn Reuben, he demonstrates his anguish by tearing his own garments and exchanging them for sackcloth—the traditional garb of mourning. While the brothers may have succeeded in ridding themselves of Joseph and deceiving their father; they now fail in their attempts to comfort him and ameliorate his sorrow. Tearfully he announces that he will mourn until the day of his death, until he *goes down* to Sheol.

Judah and Tamar (Genesis 38)

Judah has just *rescued* his brother Joseph from certain death by negotiating his sale into slavery. He now interrupts the continuation of the Joseph story with a narrative of his own fortunes in the land of Canaan. Although numerous scholars consider the narrative told in chapter 38 an intrusion, we will see that the narrative fits nicely into the larger context and interacts in telling ways both with the preceding events and especially with the following events narrated in Genesis 39.

Judah marries a Canaanite woman. By this stage in Genesis,

we readily anticipate complications. His Canaanite wife (Shua) gives him three sons—Er, Onan, and Shelah. When they come of age, he marries the oldest to a woman named Tamar (a Canaanite?). The following narration is crisp and intriguingly brief. We learn that Er was *"wicked in the sight of the LORD"* and thus put to death. We are provided no specifics regarding Er's wickedness. Though the law of levirate marriage is still in the distance, the practice is not. Judah sends his second son Onan to perform the duties of a brother and sire a child through Tamar. Though we may be well prepared for difficulties, we are surprised when we learn that Onan refuses to provide his deceased brother an heir. In contrast to Er, whose sin goes unspecified, Onan's sin is clearly detailed. Contrary to popular opinion, Onan's sin is not masturbation; it is refusal to provide a child for his deceased brother. His refusal to act on behalf of his brother effectively causes his brother's name to drop from the records. God causes a second death in Judah's family in response to Onan's obstinance. Judah, fearful that he will lose his third and final son, delays Tamar. He tells her he will send Shelah "when he grows up." Judah instructs her to return to her father's house, effectively sending her into oblivion. Tamar obeys her father-in-law.

Time passes. Judah seemingly has forgotten his promises to Tamar. In the following scene we learn that Judah has recently lost his wife and spent time in mourning. The period of mourning past, Judah goes forth to shear sheep at Timnah. Judah may have forgotten his parental obligations; Tamar has not. Like Judah, she also lays aside her garments of widowhood, exchanging them for the garb of a prostitute. Ironically, she waits for Judah at the gate of Enaim. The text delights in the subtle wordplay. Judah is on his way to shear sheep at *Timnah* ("conceal"); he will encounter Tamar at the *entrance to Enaim* (literally, "opening of the eyes").

Judah *recognizes* the dress of the prostitute, but not the person. He negotiates the transaction—one goat. The ensuing conversation is rich with irony. This "prostitute" is unwilling to take her client at his word! She requires some pledge that he will *fulfill his commitments*. As a sign of good faith, Judah willingly complies, leaving this woman his signet ring, staff, and cord. After the soiree, Judah goes merrily on his way, while Tamar returns to the garments indicating her lamentable state—the forgotten widow. In the larger context, irony also reigns. We have ample evidence from the ancient Near East (especially Canaan and Mesopotamia) for a variety of types of prostitution. An especially noteworthy form of prostitution appeared in the religious practices of the peoples surrounding Israel. These young women (and men) received a different designation than the usual term for prostitute (*zonah*). They were called *qedesh/qedeshah*—*temple prostitute* (from the same root for "holy"). Interestingly, Judah consistently designates his actions and illicit affair with the common secular designation (*zonah; zenumim*); Hirah his Canaanite friend attempts to elevate his actions to the religious sphere by using the terms particular to that activity (*qedeshah*).

In due time, Judah fulfills his obligation. He sends a goat by his friend Hirah, but no prostitute can be found in the environs. Judah, sensing a potentially embarrassing situation, decides to let the matter drop and suffer the loss of goods. However, more problematic news arrives, news that trumps whatever concerns he might have had regarding his lost possessions. Tamar his widowed daughter-in-law is pregnant. His earlier concern over embarrassment at the loss of goods has turned to outright shame at the news of this dishonorable act by Tamar. She apparently went away, but not quietly!

Judah moves quickly to rectify the situation. We can only speculate at what thoughts might have passed through his mind. Having lost two sons with this woman, he now learns that she has become a prostitute and is pregnant! He orders her death, death by incineration. However, Judah's understanding of this situation is far from complete. Tamar willingly offers to disclose the participant in her activities. Just as Judah earlier produced (with his brothers) a bloodstained coat to see if his father could *recognize* (37:32) its owner, so now Tamar produces a signet ring, staff, and cord to see if anyone might *recognize* (38:25) their owner! When she displays Judah's goods, he can only rightfully acknowledge—"*she is more in the right than I*" (38:26). Judah's language is telling; he uses the standard Old Testament term for *righteousness* (*tsedaqah*). Tamar has creatively caused Judah to keep a commitment he apparently never intended to fulfill.

The scene closes with a fascinating account of the conclusion of her pregnancy. She delivers twins. The birth of her twins takes us back to the birth of Judah's father. The first child prepares to exit the womb, stretching out his hand first. The midwife encircles it quickly with a crimson thread, so that this firstborn status will not be lost in the confusion of the birth of both boys. However, no sooner does she do this than the child retracts his hand and the other son comes forth! The twins are rightly named—Perez ("breach") for the first-born and Zerah ("brightness"—for the crimson thread?) for the latter. Tamar finally has her long-awaited heirs. (We learn much later that Zerah and Perez become the ancestors of important families in Judah. King David will come from the lineage of Perez.)

Joseph and Potiphar's Wife (Genesis 39)

Genesis 39 returns us to Joseph. Joseph is *taken down* to Egypt. Slave trafficking was well established during these times. Egyptian records list slaves that were purchased and sold between Canaan and Egypt. Often adult slaves would keep their Semitic names; child slaves typically acquired Egyptian names. Having survived the terror of a brief sojourn in a pit (cistern), Joseph now moves quickly through the Egyptian slave market. Potiphar the Egyptian purchases Joseph.

The Joseph we meet in Genesis 39 is dramatically different from our first encounter in chapter 37. This is no spoiled brat or presumptuous favored child. Joseph behaves responsibly and wisely. He quickly and justifiably ascends to a position of prominence in Potiphar's house. Joseph's mature disposition and responsible demeanor leads Potiphar to assign Joseph a coveted position—chief steward of the household. Joseph will not experience the normal lot of a slave—life in the fields or on construction sites. He will have responsibility for everything in his master's household excepting Potiphar's most intimate relationship—his wife. The text tells us that Potiphar's *only* concern was with his own food.

More importantly, Potiphar recognizes in Joseph one blessed by God. Commentary about God's blessings has been noticeably absent in the Joseph narrative to this point. When it emerges, intriguingly we are told that the evidence for the divine blessing of Joseph is attested through the prospering of his master Potiphar. Joseph lives a somewhat dual existence. He bears the blessing of God, yet lives the life of a slave. The indicators of his blessedness come through the increase in his master's wealth and possessions!

"Now Joseph was handsome and good-looking." Joseph is the first non-female to receive such a designation. This seemingly innocent

declaration ominously announces an imminent change in Joseph's fortune. Potiphar's wife, the one "item" in the house for which Joseph is not responsible, begs Joseph to act irresponsibly and sleep with her. Joseph consistently refuses. His brother Judah may give in to his sexual urges; Joseph will not. His reason is telling:

> "Look, with me here, my master has no concern about any-thing in the house, and he has put everything that he has in my hand. He is not greater in this house than I am, nor has he kept back anything from me except yourself, because you are his wife. How then could I do this great wickedness, and sin against God?" (39:8-9, emphasis added).

Joseph refuses her advances. This is no innocent tryst; it is adultery (often called the *great sin* in the ancient world). Joseph repeatedly refuses her advances. In futile frustration, Potiphar's wife aggressively seizes Joseph and demands that he lie with her. Although he escapes her clutches, his garment does not fare so well. Once again, Joseph's garment will play a central role in the interpretation of a pivotal event in Joseph's life.

Earlier Joseph's brothers simply produced a coat and allowed their father to fill (mistakenly) in the gaps in the story; Potiphar's wife allows her husband no such leeway. She calls her attendants, produces the incriminating garment, and talks in such a way that removes any ambiguity about what has just transpired. Her husband readily accepts her depiction of the crime; Joseph, having survived one pit, now finds himself *thrown* (39:30, cf. 37:24) into another. (The same term is used for cistern and prison in chapters 37 and 39.)

Joseph the Interpreter of Dreams (Genesis 40–41)

Joseph starts over. In prison, he demonstrates the same responsible behavior previously shown to Potiphar. The chief warden quickly recognizes Joseph's diligence and maturity. He entrusts a sector of the prison to him. In Genesis 38 we saw a dramatic change in Joseph's behavior. No longer a spoiled and presumptuous brat promoting himself, he was now a responsible and mature caretaker of another's possessions. In Genesis 40, the transformation continues. Joseph is no longer the dreamer; he now becomes the *interpreter* of dreams. More importantly, he will consistently give God the credit for his ability to interpret dreams.

Into Joseph's cellblock come the royal cupbearer and baker. Having offended the Pharaoh, they are sentenced to prison. While in Joseph's care, they both have a dream. The royal butler tells Joseph his dream. When Joseph offers him a promising and positive interpretation of his dream, the baker divulges his dream. The baker receives a negative and ominous interpretation. We will not have to wait long to determine whether Joseph can interpret or not. With both he provides a time frame for their realization—three days. True to the interpretation, three days later the butler, who dreamt of plucking and squeezing grapes into the royal goblet, is released from prison and re-instated to his former position. Tragically, the baker's dream comes true as well. Having dreamt of birds plucking bread from his basket, he is summarily executed by the king.

Joseph's conversation with the royal cupbearer is most intriguing. Before the butler's departure from confinement, Joseph asks that he not forget the kindness Joseph has shown him; in fact, he asks that he mention this kindness to the Pharaoh. For the first time, Joseph provides a reason for his presence in Egypt—he was kidnapped (40:15)! At this stage, the text has us guessing concerning the extent of Joseph's knowledge about the particulars of his exile to Egypt. (Later with his brothers he will suggest another reason for his presence.) The scene concludes poignantly—no sooner did the royal cupbearer receive his old post than he *forgot* Joseph (40:23)! (The book of Exodus will open with a Pharaoh who *forgot* the kindnesses of Joseph toward the land of Egypt.)

Two years later, the king of Egypt has dreams. When none of the Egyptian magicians can interpret the dreams, the royal cupbearer suddenly regains his memory. We wonder if the king did not issue threats of imprisonment, triggering bad memories for the butler? The butler's language is noteworthy. He confesses to the king, "I remember my faults today" (41:9). Joseph is retrieved from his cell. The king repeats his two dreams in their entirety. We know we must take these dreams seriously, since *idle* dreams never come in pairs (see 41:32). The dreams are somewhat bizarre, but thematically consistent. In both the obviously weaker and inferior overcome and dominate the stronger and superior. In the first dream, ugly, thin cows devour the sleek and fat cows, with no apparent weight gain. In the second dream, thin and blighted shoots of grain devour plump and full stalks of grain.

Joseph not only interprets the royal dreams, he gives advice! With the royal cupbearer, he coupled his interpretation with a plea, a plea the butler quickly forgot. With the king, he couples his interpretation with unsolicited advice! In both cases, he attributes his interpretive abilities to God. The king is easily persuaded. He makes a phenomenal assertion for a foreign king—*"Can we find anyone else like this—one in whom is the spirit of God?"* (41:37). In a royal court teeming with a myriad assortment of magicians, sorcerers, soothsayers, fortune-tellers, and sages, the Pharaoh, himself considered divine by his fellow Egyptians, declares Joseph the true possessor of the divine spirit!

The Pharaoh ratifies his affirmation with his exaltation of Joseph to a position of pre-eminence in the empire. He not only releases Joseph from prison, he elevates him to the position of vizier (second in command). (The title is not given until 42:6.) Joseph is specifically commissioned to carry out his own advice. The Pharaoh declares that only in matters of the throne (military affairs?) will he supersede Joseph's authority. The text helps us interpret the rise and fall of Joseph's fortunes by providing indicators along the way. Joseph falls and rises twice from the pit (initially the cistern; finally prison). Further, Joseph's *change in fortune* typically is signaled by his *change in attire*. We first meet Joseph wrapped in a lavish coat. His life will change dramatically when his brothers strip him of that coat and sell him into slavery. In Egypt, his bleak conditions seemingly change for the better in Potiphar's house. He rises to a position of responsibility and prominence. However, once again his fortunes will change as he is stripped of his garment when fleeing the clutches of Potiphar's wife. Finally, his exaltation will become complete when the king of Egypt removes his prison attire and robes him in fine linen and places a signet ring on his finger and gold chain about his neck (41:42, treatment somewhat similar to that received much later by the *undeserving* prodigal son in Luke 15). Previously over Potiphar's house (except for Potiphar's food and wife), he now has under his watch the entire empire, save the throne.

Pharaoh does not miscalculate Joseph's abilities. The scene concludes with a double accounting. Professionally, Joseph strategically stockpiles grain and foodstuffs so effectively that even the notoriously proficient Egyptian accountants lose count! Personally, the king (not God) renames Joseph, giving him an Egyptian name—*Zaphenath-paneah* (meaning unknown?) and an Egyptian bride—*Asenath* (the daughter of an influential priest from Heliopolis). Professionally, Joseph's prediction of an imminent famine comes true. The severity of the famine impacts even the local Egyptians. Joseph opens the bulging warehouses for the hungry people of the land. Personally, Joseph is surrounded by Egyptian power and prestige, both royally and religiously. In the midst of such, he gives his two sons *Hebrew* names—Manasseh (*menashsheh*—"causing to forget") "for God has made me forget (*nashshani*) all my hardship and all my father's house" and Ephraim (*'ephraim*—"fruitful") "for God has made me fruitful (*haphrani*) in the land of my misfortunes."

Finding Ourselves in Genesis 37–41

From one vantage point, the Joseph narrative can almost stand alone. Though some of the names and places may initially be unfamiliar, with relative ease the story unfolds in a coherent and meaningful manner. From another vantage point, the Joseph narrative follows smoothly and is inseparably linked with the preceding patriarchal narratives. The conflict and tension arising in Jacob's life now spills over into the lives of his children. Genesis 37–50 chooses to detail the lives of the following generation from the vantage point of one son—Joseph.

We watch a marvelous transformation in Joseph take place. Joseph inspires us, for in Joseph we see a man of God move from self-absorbed presumption to faithful and judicious care for others. Joseph's life is far from smooth or devoid of difficulty. Turmoil and tension run throughout. However, through it all, we have an opportunity to see this man of God adjust and respond to the call and claim of God upon his life.

Joseph provides us with a model of faithful living, and helps us reflect upon the nature of a life lived faithfully and wisely. As the story opens (Genesis 37), Joseph himself must bear responsibility for much of the conflict and tension in his family. He repeatedly seems bent on actions that alienate him from his brothers and highlight his favored status. Not surprisingly, such actions create animosity and discord. Joseph becomes the not-so-innocent victim of his brothers' anger and hatred. When we next encounter Joseph, he is no longer a favored son singled out for preferential treatment; he is now an indentured servant. However, with the change in his *social status* has come a dramatic transformation in his *moral character*. No longer the spoiled brat, he now models wisdom, responsibility, faithfulness, and concern for the other. He responsibly discharges his household duties with dispatch and integrity. The change in Joseph's character contrasts notably with his change in circumstances. Chapter 39 presents Joseph alone—bereft of family and far from the promised land. (Joseph finds himself in Potiphar's house, not his own.) Though isolated socially, Joseph is not isolated spiritually. Strikingly, the text spends little time documenting Joseph's assessment of his lamentable circumstances. Whereas Joseph's character and behavior previously generated a negative living environment within his own family, Joseph's character and behavior now bring blessing and well-being to those he serves.

- Is it fair to characterize Joseph's early behavior as "enhancing his favored status"?
- There's a saying, "He can dish it out but he can't take it." When have you "justly" received retaliation from others for your actions?

We do well to note the implicit contrast the text makes at this point. Joseph's external social and physical conditions stand dramatically at odds with his spiritual condition. Clothing plays a fascinating role in the narrative. Whereas earlier Jacob used clothing to deceive his father Isaac, his sons use the clothing given the favorite son to deceive the father. More specifically, coats play a crucial role in the Joseph story. Joseph begins with a patrician's coat, loses it in the pit, loses another garment to Potiphar's wife, and eventually regains a patrician's coat in Egypt (as vizier). Coats document Joseph's change in fortunes! Joseph finds himself in a pit on more than one occasion—first at the hands of his brothers; next at the hands of his Egyptian master (prison). Though Joseph finds himself either enslaved or in prison throughout the next decade of his life, he thrives spiritually. Both Potiphar and the chief warden acknowledge that their success and well-being comes from Joseph. Both acknowledge the presence of God in his life. Such a message is desperately needed today. In a culture that equates blessing with external comforts and longs to receive divine favors from God, Joseph is a stark reminder that spiritual health and maturity may have little correlation with physical and social status or comfort. The narrative of Joseph, like the earlier narrative of Abraham, reminds us that God calls us primarily to bless others. Joseph remains enslaved while bringing marvelous blessings to the house of Potiphar.

Against this backdrop, the interchange between Joseph and Potiphar's wife and Judah with his daughter-in-law Tamar stands in striking contrast. At least three comparisons and contrasts occur: Judah/Joseph; Potiphar's wife/Tamar; Joseph/Tamar. Clearly Judah's absence of sexual control and failure to behave responsibly toward Tamar stands in striking contrast to Joseph's moral self-control. Judah thinks of his own needs and desires; Joseph thinks of his responsibilities toward his master Potiphar. (Sexual promiscuity among slaves was a perennial feature of ancient Near Eastern societies.) Tamar is virtually powerless to change her lamentable circumstances and is bereft of any meaningful future; she must operate creatively from a stance of desperation. In contrast, Potiphar's wife has a position of power and exploits it fully. Notably, Potiphar's wife is the only female in the book of Genesis described with power language! Finally, Joseph and Tamar act "rightly," even though their actions place them in peril.

Although interpreters often caricature the episode between Potiphar's wife and Joseph simply as a sexual escapade, we would suggest the scene is more complex. In significant ways, the scene develops the theme of power more than sex. (This is not to minimize the sexual nature of the sin. Adultery consistently is labeled the *great sin*—in Egypt as well as Israel.) Noticeably, Potiphar and his wife are consistently identified based on their social roles in life. (Potiphar's wife is the only "notable" woman in the Joseph narrative.) Potiphar's wife employs power and authority language rather than the vocabulary of seduction. Appropriately, Joseph responds less to the sexual implications than to the breach of trust in his relationship with Potiphar such activity would cause. (Ironically, while Joseph is thrown into prison without a trial; the warden quickly recognizes his integrity and entrusts a cellblock to him.) Acknowledging this aspect of the narrative carries implications for our current social conditions. In the Old Testament, adultery often appears as an abuse of power and violation of trust. Acknowledging this central element of this most prevalent sin in our contemporary society may provide new avenues for addressing the grievous social implications of such activity. In a society given to an ethical stance articulated perhaps best by *no harm, no foul,* we might rightly question whether abuse of power and violation of trust result in *no harm.*

■ Have you witnessed a similar "power play" in the work place? What are the ethical lessons for us?

A third message from the early period of Joseph's life concerns his identity. When taken to Egypt, Joseph finds himself surrounded by the allure of Egyptian culture and religion. With Joseph's rise to power and prominence in Egypt, new questions of identity arise. Will Joseph be more influenced by his new surroundings and change in fortunes, or will he retain the identity of his past? This question is not without importance. Joseph now wears a royal signet ring, a royal robe, rides in the royal chariot, and receives an Egyptian name. He is married to the daughter of a most influential priest of the powerful sun god Re. To what degree will these new circumstances impact Joseph? The pampered life he experienced as his father's favorite is far behind him. He has suffered grievously at the hands of many. Will he embrace this new life of luxury and prestige? Will he relegate the cruelties of his past treatment to a forgotten past, and fully engage his present lot in life? Simply put, will Joseph now let his physical surroundings or the divine presence dominate his worldview and outlook?

Though Joseph's circumstances have changed dramatically, the text informs us that his *true* identity has not. Joseph consistently attributes his success, most notably manifested in his ability to interpret dreams, to the God of his ancestors Abraham, Isaac, and Jacob. Though he may now be wearing the garb of Egyptian royalty, he carries the faith of his fathers deep within. This appears most notably when he names his children. His sons do not receive Egyptian names, but Hebrew names designating clearly Joseph's understanding of his past—Manasseh and Ephraim. Joseph provides us a powerful model for faithful living in the midst of a sometimes hostile, sometimes alluring culture. Whether the victim of that culture or its beneficiary, Joseph remains true to the call and claim of God upon his life. In the midst of incredible injustice, Joseph models for us Paul's affirmation in 1 Corinthians 10:13—*"God is faithful, and he will not let you be tested beyond your strength, but with the testing he will also provide the way out so that you may be able to endure it."*

Finally, the narrative of Joseph helps us reflect seriously upon the presence (and at times seeming absence) of God in our world. Numerous interpreters cite the motif of the *hiddenness of God* (providence) evident in the Joseph narrative. In comparison to the Abraham and Jacob cycles, the Joseph cycle is noticeably lacking *overt* divine activity. Unlike Abraham and Jacob, Joseph receives no divine visits. On an initial read, God seems *almost* absent. References to God in the Joseph narrative are worth noting. There are approximately 50 references to God in the narrative; many of them derive from Joseph himself (for example, when he credits God with his ability to interpret dreams). Strikingly, though God may seem *absent* in the story, Joseph speaks of him repeatedly. He is *present* most clearly through Joseph's speech and behavior. Perhaps most significantly, in the entire Joseph narrative God is said to be *with Joseph* only twice—in Potiphar's house and in prison! Precisely at those moments in Joseph's life when God might appear most absent, God's presence is affirmed.

It is against this backdrop that the presence of God should be read. Though far removed from the promises to Abraham, we read that Potiphar's house experiences the fullness of the Lord's blessings (39:5)! Though Joseph may appear in less than "blessed" circumstances, he is blessing those with whom he comes in contact. Joseph's responsible behavior allows Potiphar to entrust his entire household affairs to this servant.

- How can your circumstances change without impacting your true identity?
- Have you been tempted to disguise your Christian faith in order to blend in with the crowd?
- How can it be true that God is "present" in his absence? What lessons do you see in this concept?

In these chapters we gain a clear perspective on the nature of God's *presence* and *activity*. With respect to God's presence, the text reminds us that the divine presence has little to do with external circumstances or location. Though Joseph finds himself far removed from the land of promise, and in dire straits, God is graciously present with him. Further, God's presence may at times be less than spectacular or even obvious. The Lord's presence does not guarantee us immunity from unjust treatment; God's providence certainly does not function as a "get out of jail free" card. Against this backdrop, the question of the nature and scope of God's activity surfaces. Though the blessings of God seem noticeably *absent* from Joseph's life, they are noticeably *present* in the life of Potiphar. Both Potiphar and the warden recognize the obvious presence of God in the life of Joseph. Joseph tangibly manifests the outworking of the promise God made to Abraham—*"through you all the families of the earth shall be blessed."* Though Joseph may not currently evidence the trappings of a blessed life, through his integrity and fidelity to the promises of God he brings blessing to the lives of others! Perhaps no message is more pertinent to modern believers. In an age when followers of God seem obsessed with *receiving* the blessings of God, the text points us to the importance of living lives given to *dispensing* the blessings of God! Joseph powerfully models for us a life transformed from self-absorption (a life that generated conflict and disunity) to a life given in service to others. Such a life God faithfully blesses. Two passages capture the essence of Joseph's life and our lives as bearers of the promise of God

> But the LORD was with Joseph and showed him steadfast love [chesed]; he gave him favor in the sight of the chief jailer (Genesis 39:21).

> What then are we to say about these things? If God is for us, who is against us? He who did not withhold his own Son, but gave him up for all of us, will he not with him also give us everything else? Who will bring any charge against God's elect? It is God who justifies. Who is to condemn? It is Christ Jesus, who died, yes, who was raised, who is at the right hand of God, who indeed intercedes for us. Who will separate us from the love of Christ? Will hardship, or distress, or persecution, or famine, or

Life In and Out of the Pit

nakedness, or peril, or sword? As it is written,

"For your sake we are being killed all day long; we are accounted as sheep to be slaughtered." No, in all these things we are more than conquerors through him who loved us. For I am convinced that neither death, nor life, nor angels, nor rulers, nor things present, nor things to come, nor powers, nor height, nor depth, nor anything else in all creation, will be able to separate us from the love of God in Christ Jesus our Lord (Romans 8:31-39).

With respect to God's presence, the text reminds us that the divine presence has little to do with external circumstances or location. Though Joseph finds himself far removed from the land of promise, and in dire straits, God is graciously present with him. Further, God's presence may at times be less than spectacular or even obvious. The Lord's presence does not guarantee us immunity from unjust treatment; God's providence certainly does not function as a "get out of jail free" card.

CHAPTER 10

"You Meant to Do Me Evil; God Meant to Do Me Good"

(Genesis 42–50)

*I*t was the best of times; it was the worst of times." So begins a famous novel, but it could equally open the closing scenes of the book of Genesis. The final chapters of Genesis not only neatly wrap up the Joseph narrative; they also prepare us for the beginning of the book of Exodus. The chapters are filled with ironic allusions looking in both directions. Joseph's brothers who sold him into Egyptian slavery come to Egypt to buy grain from their brother. They do not recognize their brother; his identity remains an issue throughout. This brother, left alone in a dry cistern while his brothers sat down to eat, will once more dine alone while his brothers eat. Jacob, the old deceiver, will experience a final deception at the hands of his sons.

The story is undoubtedly a literary masterpiece. For those unfamiliar with the story, it presents numerous twists, turns, and potential wrong endings. Like a masterful play, heroes and villains abound. We turn each page with suspense, wondering if the present dilemma will find a successful resolution. For those of us who have heard this story many times, it also intrigues us, for with each reading we notice elements and subtle nuances previously unnoticed. The artistry of the narrative has us constantly rewinding and fast-forwarding the story in our minds. For us, the outcome is well known; what we notice are those seemingly innocent details that now carry so much meaning. Ultimately, we will see that the literary artistry of the materials is only surpassed by its theological power. The final chapters of Genesis bring squarely before us two great theological themes—the providence of God and reconciliation.

The closing chapters of the Joseph narrative move back and forth between Canaan and Egypt. Although there are numerous minor scenes, the final chapters of Genesis consist of three major scenes: Joseph and his brothers (Genesis 42–44); a family reunion (Genesis 45–47); final blessings (Genesis 48–50).

Joseph and His Brothers (Genesis 42–44)

With chapter 42, the plot thickens. Having tracked the fortunes of Joseph for several scenes, we now return to chapter 37. True to his interpretation, a severe famine breaks out. Our familiarity with the ancient Near East allows us to anticipate that with drought and the ensuing famine, pilgrimages will be made to Egypt to secure food.

Genesis 42 begins with a simple wordplay; wordplays run throughout the narrative. When Jacob *learns* (literally, "sees") that Egypt has grain for sale, he chides his sons for their inaction. To paraphrase, he asks them why they continue *to look at each other* (literally, "see") and not journey forth to Egypt to buy grain? The sons saddle up and head south to Egypt to secure food.

The scene shifts to Egypt. Joseph, architect of the plan to survive this severe famine, administers directly the sale of food to Egyptians and foreigners. When Joseph sees his brothers come to purchase grain, he immediately *recognizes* them, though they do not recognize him. We are not surprised, for the previous scene has prepared us for such an occurrence. Joseph now *looks* fully Egyptian; he wears expensive Egyptian attire and sports an Egyptian haircut. In contrast, his brothers still bear the look of Canaanite shepherds.

Joseph initiates the transaction with a seemingly innocent series of questions about their origins and family history. They come before him and bow; Joseph remembers his first dream of Genesis 37. We cannot help but wonder how that memory will affect him. The answer comes quickly. He accuses them of espionage, charging that their supposed grain expedition is simply a ruse to determine the vulnerability of the land. (Joseph uses language of sexual violation—"nakedness of the land"—highlighting the seriousness of their alleged journey.) To prove their innocence, they detail their larger family history. They affirm their mission is simply one of survival—they are merely sons sent by their father to purchase grain. Their father and youngest brother remain in Canaan awaiting their return.

Joseph responds decisively. To determine the veracity of their story, he decides to imprison all but one son. That son will return to Canaan and bring the youngest son to Egypt as proof! He imprisons them for three days. These brothers who earlier placed their brother in a pit (cistern) now find themselves "innocent" victims in a pit (prison)! We immediately remember the plight of the royal cupbearer and baker who came to Joseph with dreams. Each of their dreams involved three more days in prison. The butler experienced liberation and restoration to his old position after three days; the baker experienced death at the end of three days. We wonder what the fate of the brothers will be in three days?

Three days later, they are released. Joseph reverses his position, allowing all but one brother to exit Egypt, because Joseph "fears God" (42:18). For the first time we hear the brothers take responsibility for their earlier mistreatment of Joseph. They acknowledge that their current plight is the consequence of their misdeeds.

> *"Alas, we are paying the penalty for what we did to our brother; we saw his anguish when he pleaded with us, but we would not listen. That is why this anguish has come upon us"* (42:21).

Reuben defensively chimes in with a less than helpful "I told you so." There will now be a "reckoning for his (i.e., Joseph's) blood" (language reminiscent of Cain and Abel).

The narrative is masterfully constructed. Joseph has yet to play his hand. All indicators point to revenge and "payback" time. Joseph stands strategically poised to right the wrongs his brothers committed against him. Their callous treatment surely deserves retribution. The scene is laced with irony. The brothers consider their plight dangerous and are fearful of the harm this suspicious Egyptian lord might inflict upon them. Little do they know that their circumstances may be more dangerous than they suppose! This is no capricious Egyptian governor before whom they stand; this is none other than their wronged brother! They are completely unsuspecting, for Joseph consistently engages them through an interpreter.

Wordplays abound in this scene. They agree to follow Joseph's instructions (literally, "they did so"—*ken*) because they told Joseph they were "honest men" (*kenim*). Reuben chides them for failure to "listen" (*shema`tem*) to him; they decide to leave Simeon (*shim`on*—"[God] has listened") behind as surety of their honesty. Joseph cannot emotionally endure the conversation; he turns away and weeps. With this scene, the text begins to offer us a glimpse into Joseph's heart. Though outwardly he may seem distant and calculating, we realize there is much more. His grief is followed quickly by his placement of their money in their grain sacks, causing us to speculate that retaliation may not carry the day.

The brothers, on their journey home, draw no such conclusions. When one brother opens his sack on the return trip and discovers money, they all react with dismay and panic. The rest will wait until they are safely home to check their sacks. They arrive home with their money, but without Simeon! (We wonder how they felt on a much earlier return to their father when they arrived with the money gained from their sale to the Ishmaelites, but minus a brother?)

The brothers recount their nightmarish adventure to their father. They detail the stipulations of any return expedition to Egypt to purchase food. Jacob responds solely from his own vantage point. He seems unconcerned about the dangers they have just experienced. He talks only of his own loss; he first lost his favorite son Joseph, he now has lost Simeon, he rejects any suggestion that he lose another son (Benjamin). Reuben rashly promises his father that he will engage the lives of his own two sons if any harm comes to Benjamin. The promise is poignant—Reuben, unable to protect Joseph from his brothers' evil devices, now pledges to his father he will protect Benjamin from a suspicious and hostile foreign potentate!

The famine rages on; the food runs out. Jacob commissions his sons to return to Egypt to purchase grain. This time his son Judah reminds him of the conditions for return. Without Benjamin, their trip will be futile. The scene again echoes Genesis 37. Judah, the architect of the initial sale of his brother Joseph, now ups the ante of his brother Reuben. Where Reuben presumptuously offered his sons as surety for Benjamin, Judah more appropriately offers his own life. In Egypt, Reuben blamed his brothers for not listening to him concerning Joseph. Now, Judah blames his father for their desperate circumstances. He retorts that his father Jacob has allowed enough time to expire to make two trips!

Jacob concedes, giving his sons explicit instructions. With a twist of irony, they are to carry local delicacies (fruits and nuts) from their land, along with gum, resin, and balm, goods the Ishmaelite caravan carried to Egypt. They also will take double the money found in their sacks; whatever profit they made selling Joseph into Egyptian slavery will now be liquidated to save themselves! Jacob sends them forth with a final prayer—he prays that God Almighty

(*El Shaddai*) will show them mercy on their journey and return both his sons (Simeon and Benjamin) to him. The die is cast; the question lingers—how will Jacob's prayer fare in a foreign land?

When they arrive, Joseph "sees" Benjamin with his brothers and instructs his steward to bring the brothers to his chambers. All the anxiety and apprehension of the first journey return. They can only assume he discovered the missing money and intends to inflict retribution. Upon entering his house, they attempt a pre-emptive strike. They immediately blurt out the strange circumstances surrounding the found money and offer it back. Joseph's response is noteworthy and anticipates his later response to them: *"Rest assured, do not be afraid; your God and the God of your fathers must have put treasure in your sacks for you; I received your money"* (43:23).

He next returns Simeon to them and invites them to dine with him. While the servants prepare the meal, the brothers prepare their gifts.

When Joseph arrives, they bow. In fact, they bow twice (43:26, 28), just as they bowed twice in Joseph's dreams (Genesis 37)! Joseph, earlier sent to inquire of his *brothers' welfare* (*shalom*—37:4), now inquires about their welfare (*shalom*) and that of his father— *"Is your father well [shalom], the old man of whom your spoke? Is he still alive?"* (43:27). Seeing his younger brother Benjamin, Joseph exclaims, *"God be gracious to you, my son!"* (43:29) Jacob's prayer is in its initial stages of fulfillment. On their first visit, Joseph had to turn from his brothers to hide his tears; now he retires to another room to hide his tears of joy. The scene closes most poignantly. In Genesis 37, the brothers sat down to dine while Joseph sat alone in a cistern. Now, Joseph sits apart from his brothers while they eat. Joseph instructs his servants to send portions from his royal table to his brothers; intriguingly, Benjamin is sent fivefold portions!

As the brothers prepare for their departure following a successful expedition to Egypt, they surely must have felt elation. They have more than enough provisions to survive the famine, they have successfully retrieved Simeon, and they are returning home with the apple of their father's eye—Benjamin. Their money has gone farther than they could have imagined. Their troubles apparently behind them, they head home.

Little do they realize their troubles are only beginning. No sooner do they clear the city limits than the police overtake them.

They are charged with a most serious offense—theft of the royal goblet, the goblet used for divination purposes. The brothers rightly express shock at such a ludicrous charge. They have just offered money mistakenly placed in their sacks from their previous expedition. Sure of their innocence, they pronounce a death sentence upon the one in whose sack the royal cup appears.

The scene is rich with meaning. As the story unfolds, we cannot help but remember an earlier account in which a search was conducted to find stolen goods. The brothers' language is hauntingly similar to that of their father's decades earlier when he slipped away from the greedy clutches of his father-in-law Laban. Jacob, oblivious to Rachel's theft of her father's idols of divination, pronounced death upon anyone who might have the stolen goods. That search moved from eldest to youngest, culminating at Rachel's tent. Surely the stolen *teraphim* would be found. However, Rachel executed an act of deception to perfection. The stolen goods remained secure in the one location Laban did not search.

Now, the brothers, not privy to the earlier actions of Rachel's favorite son (Joseph), pronounce death upon the holder of the Egyptian vizier's divination cup. The search moves dramatically from oldest to youngest. This time no deception occurs, for Benjamin and his brothers are unknowing victims of a royal plot! Benjamin is arrested; the brothers all return to Egypt.

When they enter once again Joseph's house, Judah steps forward as the spokesman. The moment is dramatic and filled with double entendre. Joseph declares their crime is folly—he can practice divination without the goblet (something we know all too well from his previous interpretations of dreams)! Joseph expresses no interest in detaining the brothers; they can depart in *peace* (*shalom*) to their homeland (44:17). While Joseph speaks of the guilt concerning the theft of the royal goblet, Judah speaks of their long-standing guilt concerning their former treatment of their brother Joseph. Both talk of guilt, but of entirely different crimes! Judah next rehearses the family history, highlighting the *welfare* of their father. Judah movingly highlights the precarious nature of their aged father's welfare. Having earlier in his life lost his dearest son, he now will surely not survive the loss of the son that replaced Joseph. Judah remains true to the promise he made to his father—he offers his life in exchange for Benjamin's release. This is certainly a different Judah from the one encountered previously. He laces his language with that servant language. No longer interested in "turning a profit," he now willingly initiates his own sale into Egyptian slavery. Earlier language that bristled with jealousy and discord is replaced by language of compassion as he speaks of his father's love for Joseph and later Benjamin. He even recalls the painful practice of his father who reserves paternal and filial language only for Rachel's sons! Judah makes one final desperate plea—"For how can I go to my father if the boy is not with me? I fear to see the suffering that would come upon my father" (44:34).

A Family Reunion (Genesis 45–47)

Genesis 45 (and 50) are to the Joseph cycle what Genesis 22 (the binding of Isaac) is to the Abraham cycle and Genesis 28 and 32 (the dream at Bethel and wrestling match at the Jabbok) are to the Jacob cycle. Joseph previously has excused himself from the presence of his brothers when overcome with emotion. He now excuses his servants. No longer able to control himself, he discloses his true identity to his brothers. He is not an *Egyptian* vizier, he is the brother they sold into slavery. Joseph's disclosure speech captures the essence of this section of material.

> "I am your brother, Joseph, whom you sold into Egypt. And now, do not be distressed, or angry with yourselves, because you sold me her; for **God sent me before you to preserve life.** For the famine has been in the land these two years; and there are five more years in which there will be neither plowing nor harvest. **God sent me before you to preserve a remnant on earth,** and to keep alive for you many survivors. **So it was not you who sent me here, but God;** he has made me a father to Pharaoh, and lord of all his house and ruler over all the land of Egypt" (45:4b-8, emphasis added).

Earlier the brothers had used servant language to define their stance before this anonymous Egyptian vizier. Now Joseph fully exploits language befitting his position and power. At one and the same time, Joseph articulates his dual identity—vizier of Egypt and estranged brother. He talks of the past; he instructs them about the future. We now receive the full disclosure of Joseph's identity.

His relationship as brother and son of Jacob will trump his position as vizier. He will utilize his position as Egyptian viceroy to preserve his family's future and insure its well-being.

When the Pharaoh discovers the identity of these migrants from Canaan, he instructs Joseph about the future. Where Joseph acknowledged God's providential guiding of his past history, the Pharaoh talks of Joseph and his family's future. The famine has only begun. Five severe years remain. He dispatches wagons to Canaan to retrieve the belongings of Joseph's extended family. The circle is almost complete—the one who entered Egypt years earlier as a powerless and vulnerable slave now enjoys the full power and prestige of Egypt. In the midst of severe destitution, Joseph is magnanimous. For the last time in Genesis, clothing will document the change in fortunes. Joseph provides his brothers new garments; his brother Benjamin receives five garments! Benjamin repeatedly receives preferential treatment; however, reconciliation rather than animosity will reign supreme. Clothing that formerly symbolized favoritism and generated discord now symbolizes restored relationships.

The wagons are loaded; Jacob will depart the land of promise one final time. He must see his favorite son, the one now favored by the Egyptians. This time exiting to the south, he stops at Beersheba, the old domicile of his father Isaac. At Beersheba he receives a revelation from his God, just as formerly he received divine assurance at Bethel (Genesis 28:10-22). God may have seemed hidden during the trials of Joseph; he is once again visibly present with Jacob.

> God spoke to Israel in visions of the night, and said, "Jacob, Jacob." And he said, "Here I am." Then he said, "I am God, the God of your father; do not be afraid to go down to Egypt, for I will make of you a great nation there. I myself will go down with you to Egypt, and I will also bring you up again; and Joseph's own hand shall close your eyes" (46:2-4).

Jacob's own vision of his future has been transformed. Whereas he thought he would only encounter Joseph when he *went down* to Sheol (37:35), God declares he will reunite with Joseph when he *goes down* to Egypt. God affirms that though Jacob is leaving the land of promise, he is not leaving the Abrahamic promise. (This may be the implicit intent of the language—"I will make of you a great nation *there*"—the tragic conditions of Abraham will not recur.) Jacob's entire entourage migrates south to Egypt.

Judah goes ahead to prepare the entrance into Egypt. Jacob and his family arrive in the northeastern sector of the Nile Delta— a region known as Goshen (later known as the land of Ramses). (Goshen may designate the land of the Hyksos, a group of foreign invaders who ruled Egypt during the second millennium and located the center of their rule in the Delta.) Joseph knows Egyptian life only too well. Egypt is a land of agriculture; roaming flocks of sheep and goats irreparably damage fertile fields. During a famine, this is no time to further deplete the precious agricultural resources. Joseph skillfully negotiates prime pastureland in the region his family has just entered. Goshen is marvelously suited as a dwelling for Jacob's family. It has suitable pasturage, it is close to Joseph, yet sufficiently distant from the heavily congested Egyptian population centers. (The narrative implicitly anticipates the strategic benefit of this location when the fortunes turn dramatically for the worse in the book of Exodus and Jacob's descendants must flee Egypt.)

When Jacob meets Pharaoh, the theological journey comes full circle. Like Abraham with Lot, Pharaoh tells Joseph that *"the land of Egypt is before you; settle your father and your brothers in the best part of the land"* (47:6). When the Pharaoh meets Jacob, Jacob himself now narrates his life story. He is 130 years old; his life has been difficult and fraught with peril. His life has seemingly been endless turmoil, from familial conflict to loss of children. The next move surprises. Jacob blesses Pharaoh! An earlier Pharaoh had almost suffered disastrous calamity at the hands of Jacob's grandfather; Jacob now brings blessing to the royal court.

With the descendants of Jacob safely settled in Egypt, the text returns to the ravaging effects of the famine. Joseph's original commission as secretary of agriculture was to insure the welfare of the Egyptian state and people. The famine has raged long and hard. Local Egyptians must repeatedly return to Joseph to secure further supplies. Their monies depleted, they now exchange livestock for food. The famine continues. Penniless and bereft of assets, they return a final time on the brink of starvation. In a desperate move, they offer their land in exchange for food. Joseph the judicious administrator ably negotiates a strategic land transaction. He purchases the land, then conscripts the former landowners to farm their previously owned property. The land belongs to the Pharaoh, but the previous landowners may now retain 80% of the goods they raise. The text cannot avoid noting the irony of this transaction—a Hebrew, formerly a *slave* of the Egyptians, now enslaves the Egyptians! (When the book of Exodus opens, the enslavement will have dramatically shifted once again from the Egyptians to the Hebrews.)

Final Blessings (Genesis 48–50)

The book of Genesis closes with blessing. The final three chapters record the blessings pronounced by the patriarch Jacob at the end of his life. The formerly robust and wily Jacob now must be helped in and out of the wagon. Like his father Isaac, his eyesight dims with age. At the close of Genesis 47, Jacob secures a promise from his favorite son Joseph that he will not be buried in the land of Egypt. Joseph promises that he will return his father's body to the cave Abraham purchased at Machpelah.

Genesis 48 details the blessing of Joseph's sons Manasseh and Ephraim. Though the blessing departs from the usual script, we are no longer surprised. Jacob first claims these two sons of Jacob for himself. He designates them his sons; they will have status equal (if not superior) to Reuben and Simeon. Jacob has still not recovered from the loss of his favorite wife Rachel; these two sons of her prized son will alleviate that loss.

Jacob apparently spends the bulk of his day on his (death)bed. When Joseph brings his two sons forward, he appropriately positions them so that the older may receive the inheritance rights (from the right hand). (We saw Joseph's earlier concern for the firstborn in his seating of his brothers—43:33). However, Jacob, ever the younger son, crosses his hands and pronounces the blessing of firstborn on the younger son Ephraim. He then pronounces the following blessing:

> The God before whom my ancestors Abraham and Isaac walked, the God who has been my shepherd all my life to this day, the angel who has redeemed me from all harm, bless the boys; and in them let my name be perpetuated, and the name of my ances-

tors Abraham and Isaac; and let them grow into a multitude on the earth" (48:15-16).

When Joseph protests the placement of his father's hands, Jacob announces that Ephraim will surpass his older brother in stature and importance. Joseph's favored status results in his lineage receiving a double portion. (This occurs when the later descendants of Jacob exit Egypt and enter the land of promise. The descendants of Ephraim and Manasseh receive land allotments equal to Jacob's other sons.)

Genesis 49 recounts Jacob's final words to his sons. Although often called the *blessings of Jacob*, this chapter in reality details the *futures* of Jacob's several sons. Some of the pronouncements are succinct and to the point, others are lengthy and complex. Most are riddled with wordplays. In some instances the past history of the son will have a determinative (negative) impact on the future of his descendants (e.g., Reuben). In other cases the descendants will enjoy the fruits of their fathers' blessing. The sons of Leah and Rachel receive more extensive commentary from their father than the sons of the handmaids, Bilhah and Zilpah. Jacob cites Reuben's indiscretion and lack of self-control as the controlling feature for his descendants' later history. Simeon and Levi, given to violence, will bequeath the consequences of their actions to their descendants. Judah stepped forward during the tenuous moments of interchange with Joseph; his descendants will benefit from such leadership and produce prominent rulers. Joseph's descendants will experience fertility and abundance. Genesis 49 provides valuable commentary to the later histories of the descendants of Jacob.

Genesis 50 recounts the death of Jacob and his return to Canaan for burial. Like Egyptian royalty, Jacob is embalmed and mourned for 70 days. In contrast to an interchange between a Pharaoh and a Hebrew that will soon follow in the book of Exodus, Joseph is immediately granted permission to leave Egypt and transport his father to Canaan for burial. After the body of Jacob is safely entombed in the burial site Abraham purchased from the Hittites, the contingent of Jacob's descendants returns to Egypt.

Genesis 50:15-21 provides a final glimpse into the tenuous relationship between Joseph and his brothers. With their father's death, the fear of the brothers returns. Perhaps Joseph has simply been *bid-*

ing his time until his father's death to seek revenge. Perhaps he did not want to bring further sorrow to his father by retaliating against his brothers during his father's lifetime. Filled with anxiety, the brothers approach Joseph after their father's death.

> *Realizing that their father was dead, Joseph's brothers said, "What if Joseph still bears a grudge against us and pays us back in full for all the wrong that we did to him?" So they approached Joseph, saying, "Your father gave this instruction before he died, 'Say to Joseph: I beg you, forgive the crime of your brothers and the wrong they did in harming you.' Now therefore please forgive the crime of the servants of the God of your father." Joseph wept when they spoke to him. Then his brothers also wept, fell down before him, and said, "We are here as your slaves." But Joseph said to them, "Do not be afraid! Am I in the place of God?* **Even though you intended to do harm to me, God intended it for good,** *in order to preserve a numerous people, as he is doing today. So have no fear; I myself will provide for you and your little ones." In this way he reassured them, speaking kindly to them* (50:15-21, emphasis added).

When Joseph first revealed his identity to his brothers (Genesis 45), he used language of royalty and emphasized the purposes of God in his life. The brothers now emphasize the instructions his father Jacob gave on his deathbed. They acknowledge their crimes against Joseph and beg forgiveness. (The terms sin and evil occur four times in the short space of seven verses.) Once again, Joseph weeps. (Language reminiscent of the earlier reconciliation between Jacob and Esau appears.) Joseph's response mentions nothing of his status in the Egyptian court; he speaks only of the place and role of God in his life. Joseph promises to protect and provide for his brothers and their children. He reassures them.

Genesis closes with the children of Jacob living in reconciled relationship in Egypt. The final comments of Joseph to his brothers return us to the beginning of Genesis. We began with the serpent challenging Adam and Eve to eat of the tree of knowledge of good and evil. In so eating they would take the place of God and determine for themselves good and evil. We close with the wise Joseph responding, *"Am I in the place of God? Though you planned evil against me, God meant it for good."* Joseph demonstrates for us a life lived wisely in right relationship with God, a life given to reconciliation rather than revenge, forgiveness rather than faultfinding, and compassion rather than cruelty.

Finding Ourselves in Genesis 42–50

In Genesis 45:4-8 Joseph reveals his true identity to his brothers. Genesis 50:15-21 records the dialogue between Joseph and his brothers following the death of their father. Although some interpreters consider the two texts unnecessary duplication, I would suggest the two texts function somewhat differently and each offer rich insights.

Genesis 45 recounts an extraordinary scene. The sons of Jacob, having come from a land engulfed in famine and death, entrusted their future to the goodwill of an unpredictable viceroy of Egypt (chapters 42–44). For them, a worst-case scenario has begun to unfold. The favorite son of their aging father has been arrested, an innocent victim of trumped-up charges. Standing before the viceroy, and surely thinking matters could not get any worse, they now hear this vizier announcing his *other* identity! He is not only viceroy of Egypt; he is their brother! The ensuing speech from Joseph is remarkable (vv. 4-8). He spends no time detailing his misadventures and tragedies. Rather, he focuses solely upon God's purpose in bringing him to Egypt for necessary future action. Joseph, their brother, continues to function as viceroy. He instructs them to return to their father, move the entire family to Egypt, and allow him to provide for them there. His language reflects the royal status to which he has risen. (Note the language—*"He [i.e., God] has made me a father to Pharaoh and lord of all his house and ruler over all the land of Egypt . . . God has made me lord of Egypt . . . I will provide for you there . . . you must tell my father how greatly I am honored in Egypt."*) The conversation is one way—the brothers do no talking.

■ When asked to forgive others have you been tempted to recite the list of wrongs before granting forgiveness? What does that reveal about your sincerity?

Once again we see the impact a faithful life has upon others. When Pharaoh receives the report that Joseph's brothers have come to Egypt, he makes a magnanimous offer of his own resources for the move to Egypt (vv. 16-20)! This is especially noteworthy, given the later Pharaonic treatment of Jacob's family by *"one who did not know Joseph and all he had done for Egypt"* (Exodus 1). Genesis 46:1-4 links closely with 45:3-8. As Jacob departs the land of promise, he offers sacrifices at Beersheba. He also receives confirmation of the Abrahamic promise:

> *God spoke to Israel in visions of the night, and said, "Jacob, Jacob." And he said, "Here I am." Then he said, "I am God, the God of your father; do not be afraid to go down to Egypt, for I will make of you a great nation there. I myself will go down with you to Egypt, and I will also bring you up again; and Joseph's own hand shall close your eyes"* (46:2-4).

Not unexpectedly, the larger scene closes somewhat ironically. Genesis 47:13-26 informs us that the landless descendants of Jacob have become an independent and flourishing community in Egypt (with land), while the native Egyptians have become landless slaves!

■ What difference can one life make? Do you believe that you are making an impact for Christ? How?
■ If Jacob knew what would happen to his family in Egypt, do you think he would have left Canaan? Is there a faith lesson for us?

Genesis 50, though in some ways an echo of Genesis 45, presents a significant scene change. Jacob the father, a father partially responsible for fostering the sibling conflict that brought the descendants of Abraham to Egypt, has died. Upon Joseph's return from the burial, his brothers anxiously ask for a hearing, fearful he still bears a grudge against them. Perhaps the death of their father will now release Joseph to avenge old grievances and settle old scores. Whereas the brothers were silent in Genesis 45, they now speak openly and present their case eloquently. They express their case in a most arresting manner. They open their appeal, not with their own request, but with a request from their dead father! They inform

Joseph that their father "gave these instructions before he died." The paternal instructions request that Joseph *"forgive the crime of his brothers and the wrong they did in harming him."* Only then do they echo this request for forgiveness, designating themselves not as brothers, but as *"servants of the god of your father."* They conclude their appeal with a profession of servitude—*"we are here as your slaves."*

The language is striking and fitting. In Genesis 45, Joseph gave instructions and, although their brother, spoke primarily as viceroy of Egypt. Further, his instructions focused almost entirely around care and concern for his father. Having followed his earlier instructions, they now beg Joseph to receive his own father's instructions. During their request, Joseph begins to weep (as in chapter 45) and utters a most marvelous response:

> *"Do not be afraid! Am I in the place of God? Even though you intended to do harm to me, God intended it for good, in order to preserve a numerous people, as he is doing today. So have no fear; I myself will provide for you and your little ones."* In this way he **reassured them, speaking kindly to them** (50:19-21, emphasis added).

At the close of Genesis 45, we have no doubt that Joseph and the sons of Jacob are sons of the same father; at the close of Genesis 50 we know they are brothers. Given the new circumstances in which Joseph and his brothers find themselves, Joseph rejects the language of royalty and embraces language of relationship.

■ Since the church is God's family, how can we treat each other the way Joseph treated his brothers?
■ How does "position" affect the way we treat one another? Can you cite some remedies for this?

While some biblical texts seem almost impossibly obscure, Genesis 45 and 50 are models of clarity. The difficulty lies not in understanding, but in implementation. These texts provide us with powerful messages relevant to our contemporary lives. I will simply note three: the nature of faith; the nature of reconciliation (and its implications for community); divine/human agency (the "plan" of God).

Joseph embodies and articulates for us the essence of faith. Faith is less about the future and more about the past. Simply put, faith is seeing not only the *human* hand in history, but also the *divine* hand. Joseph looks back over his life and affirms that not only have humans been involved in his history (for good and ill), but also more importantly, God has been involved (always for good). The life of Joseph reminds us that things are not always what they seem. In a most unexpected fashion, the Lord uses a famine as a means of preserving his people! Joseph's own life, though often seemingly tenuous and riddled with misfortune, plays a role in changing the behavior of those around him and provides a meaningful future for others. The story of Joseph reminds us that sometimes we find ourselves in situations where the overriding concern is with the preservation of life itself! Joseph reminds us that in the midst of our most difficult circumstances, God may use us powerfully to preserve life. Such is the nature of faith. Joseph embodies the conviction of Isaiah 40:29-31:

> *He gives power to the faint,*
> *and strengthens the powerless.*
> *Even youths will faint and be weary,*
> *and the young will fall exhausted;*
> *but those who wait for the LORD shall*
> *renew their strength,*
> *they shall mount up with wings like eagles,*
> *they shall run and not be weary,*
> *they shall walk and not faint.*

Genesis 45 and 50 provide us with an important *case study* in reconciliation. If we are honest, Joseph's situation in Genesis 45 is one we long for! Having been the victim of injustice and abuse, he now "holds all the cards." Inviting options present themselves to him. He can opt for revenge; he can scold and lecture; he can even offer grace and forgiveness while still maintaining power and authority (a favorite option today). At times a pivotal hindrance to reconciliation involves the absence of language each party wants to hear. The dialogue between Joseph and his brothers instructs us. In chapter 50, the brothers begin their appeal, not with their own confession of sin, but with an appeal to their father and a common faith.

Joseph responds by rejecting the trappings of power and authority, choosing instead language of family and vulnerability. (In Genesis 15 and 32 we see the tremendous impact divine vulnerability has upon the divine-human relationship; here we see the impact vulnerability has upon restoring human relationships.) While Joseph explicitly rejects a divine role for himself (possibly referring to their request for forgiveness and offer to become slaves), he manifests divine graciousness to his anxious brothers through his speech (*"do not be afraid"*) and reassures them of his intent to do good for them as their God has done for him. Joseph apparently recognizes the latent mistrust his brothers harbor and moves toward its removal. The Joseph story powerfully reminds us that genuine reconciliation only occurs when both parties willingly make themselves vulnerable and choose a common stance of equality before God. Only then does true community result.

■ Describe the nature of faith according to Isaiah 40.
■ List the steps of reconciliation from Genesis 50.
■ If you make yourself vulnerable to others yet equal before God, does this imply weakness? Why or why not?

A final theme concerns the relation of the divine and human in effecting the plan of God. An obvious first step involves the recognition and affirmation that God does indeed have a plan for his creation and his people. Second, humans are neither mere puppets in this plan, nor do they have the power ultimately to thwart the divine plan. The Joseph story reminds us that our lives are part of a divine—human drama, a drama in which both parties influence and are influenced, and both can resist and be resisted. Like Joseph, humans can exhibit and effect good in the midst of evil. Like the brothers, humans can temporarily hinder or thwart the working of good in the world. What is beyond dispute is the final outcome. In our faith journey of finding ourselves in Genesis, we would do well to imitate the best examples and embrace the call of God. Joseph embodies Paul's affirmation in Romans 8:28:

"We know that all things work together for good for those who love God, who are called according to his purpose."

A final theme concerns the relation of the divine and human in effecting the plan of God. An obvious first step involves the recognition and affirmation that God does indeed have a plan for his creation and his people. Second, humans are neither mere puppets in this plan, nor do they have the power ultimately to thwart the divine plan. . . . Like Joseph, humans can exhibit and effect good in the midst of evil. Like the brothers, humans can temporarily hinder or thwart the working of good in the world. What is beyond dispute is the final outcome. In our faith journey of finding ourselves in Genesis, we would do well to imitate the best examples and embrace the call of God.

Suggested Book List

Below is a brief listing of books for further reading you might find helpful in your study of Genesis. The works listed approach Genesis from a variety of theological perspectives. They all attempt to relate the ancient text of Genesis and the Bible to the contemporary world.

Walter Brueggemann, *Genesis* (Interpreter's Commentary). John Knox, 1982.

Terence Fretheim, *The Pentateuch*. Abingdon, 1996.

———, Genesis (The New Interpreters Bible, edited by Walter J. Harrelson). Abingdon, 2003.

Victor Hamilton, *The Book of Genesis* 1-17, 18-50 (NICOT). 2 vols. Eerdmans, 1990, 1995.

Thomas Mann, *The Book of the Torah*. John Knox, 1988.

Foster McCurley, *Genesis, Exodus, Leviticus, Numbers* (Proclamation Commentaries). Fortress, 1979.

Bill Moyers (editor), *Genesis: A Living Conversation*. Doubleday, 1996. (Based on a PBS series Moyers produced).

Roland Murphy, *Responses to 101 Questions on the Biblical Torah: Reflections on the Pentateuch*. Paulist, 1996.

Nahum Sarna, *Understanding Genesis: The Heritage of Biblical Israel*. Schocken Books, 1966.

Gerhard von Rad, *Genesis* (Old Testament Library). Westminster, 1972.

Gordon Wenham, *Genesis 1-15, 16-50* (Word Biblical Commentary). 2 vols. Word, 1987, 1994.

Claus Westermann, *Genesis 1-11, 12-36, 37-50*. 3 vols. Augsburg, 1984, 1985, 1986.

John Willis, *Genesis* (Sweet Living Commentary). Sweet, 1979.

About the Author

Rick R. Marrs is Blanche E. Seaver Professor of Religion and Chair of the Religion Division at Pepperdine University. He received his B.A. in Koine Greek and his Master of Divinity from Abilene Christian University. He received his Ph.D. in Near Eastern Studies from Johns Hopkins University. He is the editor of *Worship and the Hebrew Bible* (JSOTS 284) and numerous scholarly articles. He serves on the journal boards of *Restoration Quarterly* and *Leaven*. At Pepperdine he teaches primarily Old Testament courses, specializing in the Prophets, Wisdom Literature, and the Psalms. He and his wife Paula live in Thousand Oaks, California, and attend the Conejo Valley Church of Christ, where he serves as an elder.